Cover: Louis XIV commode & figurines, courtesy of
Rosenberg & Stiebel; George Inness painting,
courtesy of Valley House Gallery.

Antiques
the Best of the Best

a survey of America's best historic homes and antique galleries

MARJORIE GLASS

The Krantz Company Publishers, Inc.

Acknowledgement: The author wishes to thank Randi
Sherman, manuscript editor, for her diligent research and
numerous contributions.

Library of Congress Catalogue Number

ISBN: 0-913765-01-5 cloth

ISBN: 0-913765-03-1 papercover

Manufactured in the United States of America

To my parents & Billy—

The Best of the Best

CONTENTS

BOOK II

Introduction

How the inclusions were chosen

When anyone, especially a writer, claims to have found the very best of something, a dual-edged sword is exposed. One side, and the most dangerous one, is the almost virtual certainty that something better comes along, and thus, the claim of "the best", is somewhat precarious.

With that in mind, another edge of the sword scrapes away the pleasures of looking back on your writings and necessitates the unpleasant task of continually defending past judgements.

This volume is exactly that, a past judgement, based on the ever-changing experience of discovering the joys of yesterday's artists and craftsmen. These judgements were based on a survey of nearly one thousand art and antique galleries and historic homes. These judgements were based on a few rules. The rules were actually quite simple and, I believe, will help the reader enjoy his or her own survey of what I deemed to be the best.

The rules, which govern inclusion in this volume, are:

(1) An exhibiting facility, be it a shop or gallery (I use these two terms synonymously) must be accommodating to the public; thus if a gallery is operated as a "private dealer" it will not be found in this book. (2) The dealer, or head of the gallery, is required to be a specialist in a given area (i.e. English silver, American painting, et al). The few exceptions to this rule were included based on the dealers general expertise in a wide area. (3) The "general integrity" of each gallery was taken into account before it could be included. This simply means that no galleries are included which, as far as I know, knowingly deal in merchandise that is not authentic and in most cases they guarantee authenticity in writing.

These rules were restrictive, and indeed did require the omission of a few galleries which deal in fine art and antiques.

Book I

Historic

Homes

The Bayou Bend Collection of the Museum of Fine Arts, Houston
1 Westcott St., P.O. Box 13157, Houston, TX 77019   (713)529-8773
Tuesday-Saturday: 10-11:15; Tuesday-Friday: 1:15-2:30   Closed the entire
month of August, New Year's Day, July 4, Labor Day, Thanksgiving, and
Christmas.   During the hours of operation, visitors are escorted by docents in
groups of four every 15 minutes   Admission is by reservation only.
Minimum age is 16, except on family tour days (first floor only) each second
Sunday except March and August, 1-5   No reservations are needed for family
tours.

Bayou Bend is the name of the 28-room house commissioned and built in 1928
by Ima Hogg and her two brothers Will and Mike. It was designed by architect
John F. Staub, who designed large homes for the commercial elite of Houston.
The house is a painted pink stucco structure which combines Greek revival and
Palladian design elements. It is surrounded by several acres of landscaped
gardens and is bordered on its north side by Buffalo Bayou, the major waterway
of the Houston area.

   The house contains an extremely large and good-quality collection of
American furnishings, which are arranged in rooms by periods. The Murphy
Room in the William and Mary style showcases furniture and objects from the
period 1650 to 1725. The central hall, or Philadelphia Hall, displays objects
made between 1760 and 1790, including Chippendale furniture made in that
city. The Music Room in the Federal period style presents examples of
American taste from 1790 to 1815, including a Duncan Phyfe piano made in
New York City. The most modern room is the Belter Parlor, an early Victorian
sitting room of the period 1845-1870.

   The house was originally meant to be approached from an entrance on Lazy
Lane. However, out of consideration for other residents of the street, the house
is now reached by a footbridge over Buffalo Bayou from a parking lot located on
Westcott Street off Memorial Drive. Guests are asked to arrive 15 minutes
before their scheduled tour so that they may be properly registered.

Biltmore House

Biltmore House and Gardens   1 Biltmore Plaza, Asheville, NC 28803   (704) 274-1776   Daily: 9-5 except New Year's Day, Thanksgiving, and Christmas Admission: adults $12; children 12-17 $9; children under 12 with adult no charge. All tours are self conducted.

Biltmore House is the mansion created on an estate of originally 125,000 acres by George Washington Vanderbilt, the grandson of "Commodore" Cornelius Vanderbilt. The carved limestone house was designed by master Ecole des Beaux-Arts architect Richard Morris Hunt, and was constructed from 1890 to 1895. The 35-acre formal gardens and parks which surround the house were designed by Frederick Law Olmsted, master of naturalistic landscape in America who designed New York's Central Park. The house and its gardens have been open to the public since 1930, sixteen years after Vanderbilt's death. Of the 250 rooms in the mansion, 55 are open to the public.

The mansion was designed in the style of 16th-century French chateaux, namely those of Chambord, Chenonceaux, and Blois in the Loire Valley. The overall style, called Francis I, reflects the period of transition from the French gothic into the Renaissance. The general character of the house, with its picturesque asymmetry, stair towers, and angle turrets, is medieval. The classic horizontal string courses and the mansard roofs (hipped roofs with two slopes on each side) are typically French Renaissance features.

In the Biltmore halls and galleries, visitors can see a vast number of art treasures, including architectural elements, furniture, and decorative objects, which were gathered by Vanderbilt in his European travels. Upstairs in the marble-paved Entrance Hall, there is an important set of bronzes by 19th-century Parisian artists Antoine Louis Barye, who is well represented in Vanderbilt's collection. The eclectic but harmonious group of furniture in this room includes a 16th-century Spanish iron chest, a 17th-century Flemish leather armchair, and a 19th-century American oak table.

The Palm Court contains a fountain with a statue by 19th-century Viennese sculptor Karl Bitter. Also from the 19th-century are carpets from Western Turkestan and Iran, and French bamboo and rattan furniture.

The Billiard Room, part of a suite of rooms where men relaxed and entertained themselves, contains 19th-century American oak pool and billiard tables. The leather settees and chairs, made by Morant & Co. in 1895, are copies of furniture at the 17th-century English estate, Knole. Original 17th-century furniture in the room includes an Italian Renaissance octagonal table, Portuguese stamped leather chairs, and a German carved oak cabinet. Covering the walls are numerous sporting and theatre prints after the paintings of Sir Edwin Landseer, Sir Joshua Reynolds, George Stubbs, and others.

The spacious Banquet Hall was designed to display five unique tapestries, the only known 16th-century Flemish tapestries woven from Venus and Vulcan designs. The banquet table and the two throne chairs were designed by the mansion's architect, R.M. Hunt. There are 67 18th- and 19th-century Italian arm and side chairs, statues and carvings by Karl Bitter, and brass and copper pieces of 18th- and 19th-century Dutch, Spanish, and French origin.

In the Family Dining Room, which was used for informal dining, there are various portraits of the Vanderbilt family. Samples of the Vanderbilts' china and glassware are found on the table and in the display cabinet. They include dinner service and dessert sets by the English Minton and Spode factories, Wedgewood lusterware, and Baccarat crystalware. Also on the table is a pair of 18th-century German Meissen candlesticks.

The Morning Salon is furnished with a set of 18th-century Louis XV chairs and sofa, desk, and bombe commode (a commode that swells outward and then recedes toward the bottom). A chess table with ivory chessmen once belonging to Napoleon

Mahogany highchest, Philadelphia (1760-1775). The Bayou Bend Collection (Houston).

Biltmore House (Asheville, N.C.), constructed 1890-95 for George Vanderbilt in a French Renaissance style with 250 rooms.

Walled Garden at Biltmore House containing 10,000 flowers.

Bonaparte is on display. There are prints by 16th-century German artist Albrecht Durer, 17th-century wall hangings of Cardinal Richelieu, and 18th-century French faience objects.

The Music Room, restored in French Renaissance style, was designed to display some outstanding art objects. Over the mantel designed by R.M. Hunt hangs Durer's *Triumphal Arch of Maximilian* of 1515, which consists of 92 engraved blocks. Meissen sculptor Johann Joachim Kandler modeled the 12 porcelain apostles and candlesticks in the room. There are also portraits by 16th-century artists Marcus Gheeraerts and Federico Zucchero.

The 75-foot-long Tapestry Gallery features three Brussels tapestries collectively titled *The Triumph of Virtue over Vice,* which were woven in the early 16th century and show the transition from the gothic to the Renaissance styles. Notable portraits in this room of members of the Vanderbilt family are by James McNeill Whistler, John Singer Sargent, and Giovanni Boldini. The range of furniture and decorative arts in this room is vast. Notable works include five 15th-century French gothic cupboard-credenzas, a 16th-century Spanish vargueno cabinet (a cabinet with a hinged drop front), a 17th-century Flemish cabinet with painted scenes, and three 19th-century American gate-leg tables (drop-leaf tables with flaps supported when raised by "gates" that swing out from the central section).

The Library contains over 20,000 volumes that reflect the broad interests of Vanderbilt. The 18th-century ceiling painting, *The Chariots of Aurora,* by Giovanni Antonio Pellegrini, comes from the Pisani Palace in Venice. Wood carvings and bronze sculpture by Karl Bitter are also found in this room.

On the second floor, the neoclassic Louis XVI bedroom contains 19th-century furnishings which reflect the French taste for opulence just before the Revolution. In the Living Hall, an upstairs sitting room, there are family portraits in addition to furniture and decorative arts of the 17th through the 19th centuries. In Vanderbilt's North Bedroom, decorated in the rococo style of Louis XV, one can view French savonnerie rugs (high-pile, hand-woven rugs decorated with floral and scroll designs), monogrammed English Spode porcelain toilet articles, and wall engravings by 18th-century French artists.

The Oak Sitting Room reflects the 17th-century Jacobean style. Notable items include a large ebony cabinet which was a special product of Antwerp and South Germany in the mid-17th century and a group of bronzes by mid-19th-century French sculptors Barye, Mene, and Meunier.

Vanderbilt's South Bedroom contains woodwork in the rich baroque style of Louis XIV; plaster friezes, urns, and busts by Eugene Arrondelle of the Louvre; and Spanish, Italian, and Portuguese furniture of the 18th and 19th centuries. Three guestrooms, namely the Old English Room, Chippendale Room, and Sheraton Room, each reflect a different style of English furnishings, as their names imply.

The Guest Suite Sitting Room contains a number of late 19th-century Victorian pieces, as well as furniture in an 18th-century Dutch style. In the Guest Suite Bedroom, most of the furniture is from the first half of the 18th century. Also on display are two paintings by French artist Pierre Auguste Renoir.

Downstairs, a section of the house which includes a gun room and smoking room, caters to men's activities. Another section consists of work areas, such as the laundry rooms, pantries, kitchens, and servants' rooms. There is also a guest recreational area with a gymnasium, swimming pool, bowling alley, and dressing rooms. Antiques appropriate to the function of each room are displayed.

Bowne House

The Bowne House   37-01 Bowne Street, Flushing, NY 11354   (212) 359-0528   Tuesday, Saturday, and Sunday: 2:30-4:30   Closed December 15-January 15 and Easter   Admission: $1.00   School groups free by appointment.

The oldest house in Queens, the Bowne House was built in 1661 by English-born merchant John Bowne. Bowne, who became a devout Quaker, allowed Quakers to hold meetings in his home. His arrest for permitting Quakers to meet in his home and his ultimate acquittal helped to establish religious freedom in America.

The original part of the house consists of the kitchen, two small adjoining rooms, and upstairs sleeping quarters, which have changed little since they were constructed. In 1680 John Bowne added the dining room with its pegged floors, hand-hewn beams, and fireplace. The present entrance and parlor were added by his sixth child, Samuel, one year after Bowne's death in 1695. Nine successive generations of the Bowne family lived in this house until 1945, when the Bowne House Historical Society purchased it and opened it to the public.

The house is filled with well-preserved, 17th and 18th-century furniture and artifacts, all of which were owned by the Bownes. In the living room is a hand-carved mahogany secretary with its original brass hardware, and portraits of Samuel Parsons and Mary Bowne Parsons, owners of the house in the early 19th century. A four-poster, Sheraton-style, feather bed is found in the William Penn Room. Also on view is a bed warmer (a metal pan attached to a long handle which was filled with embers and rubbed between the sheets before retiring on a cold night). The library contains a desk made by a friend of John Bowne from a fruit tree on his plantation. Family documents are displayed here as well.

The oldest part of the house, the kitchen, has been arranged to recreate the atmosphere of the time when John Bowne and his wife, Hanna occupied it. Furnishings and household items, which include a collection of pewter tableware, point to the fact that in early colonial times, the kitchen was the center of activity. Items on display were used for cooking, eating, washing, spinning, weaving, preserving food, storing various articles, and relaxing.

The dining room houses a highboy (high chest of drawers) in the William and Mary style as well as chairs of the early Queen Anne style. A tall eight-day clock, attributed to Anthony Ward in Manhattan about 1735, still keeps time. Portraits hung in this room are of Samuel Bowne (1812-90) and his wife Elizabeth Ackerly Bowne (1814-75) painted by Francois Anetti in 1835.

A single small room is used for rotating exhibits, which range from early clothing to fine china.

Breakers

The Breakers   Ochre Point Ave., c/o The Preservation Society of Newport County   118 Mill Street, Newport, RI 02840   (401) 847-1000   Daily: 10-5; July—mid-September: Tuesday-Thursday and Sunday: 10-8   Admission: adults, $4.50; children 6-11, $1.25.   Group reservations and rates are available.

The Breakers was built in 1895 for Cornelius Vanderbilt as a summer residence modeled after the great Renaissance palaces of northern Italy. Richard Morris Hunt, a master architect who studied at the Ecole des Beaux-Arts in Paris, designed this home. The colossal four-floor, 70-room building incorporates loggias, balconies, and terraces. Its formal, symmetrical composition contrasts with the French gothic, asymmetrical structure of Biltmore, designed by Hunt during the same years for Vanderbilt's brother, George.

Bowne House (Flushing, N.Y.), one of the earliest still-standing homes in America. Built circa 1690.

Bowne House Parlor.

The Great Hall, used as a reception and circulation area, is a room with opulently-carved and gilded imported French stone. The wrought-iron and bronze railing on the stairs is an outstanding example of metalwork. On display are a huge Flemish tapestry designed by Karl Van Mander in 1619, eight bronze candelabras with figures patterned after 16th-century Italian originals, and two porphery vases after those in the Salon d'Apollon at Versailles. There is a tremendous Italian Caen-stone, hooded fireplace flanked by carved mahogany sliding doors with mirrors.

The Library contains panels decorated with bas-relief carvings in the style of the High Renaissance. Bound volumes of books, mostly works of 19th-century authors such as Thackeray, Irving, and Howells, are placed in arched recesses and book cases. The 16th-century French fireplace comes from the Chateau d'Arnay-le-Duc. Among the furnishigns in the room are busts, statues, and portraits of members of the Vanderbilt family.

The Grand Salon or Music Room, used for recitals and dancing, was designed by the French architect Richard Bouwens Van der Boyen. It was constructed by the French cabinet-making firm Allard & Sons, who shipped the entire work to Newport for installation. The room's Furniture with Italian cut-velvet upholstery and gilded hardware, and the chandeliers are works designed by Van der Boyen.

Also designed by Van der Boyen, the Morning Room contains Italian Renaissance paintings of the muses on panels in the corners of the room. The gilt, upholstered furniture is copied after pieces in the Palais Correr in Venice. In the Billiard Room, a San Domingo mahogany pool table and several other

pieces of furniture were designed by Baumgarten of New York.

The magnificent, ornate Dining Room exhibits a ceiling painting, *Aurora at Dawn.* Decorating the walls and ceiling are red alabaster columns with bronze Corinthian panels, gilt moldings, cornices, garlands, and neoclassical lifesize figures in the ceiling arches. The Family Dining Room or Breakfast Room is finished in antique paneling taken from a house in France at the time of Louis XV (1715-74), who was best known for a rococo style of decoration. The marble mantel piece and mahogany furniture decorated with gilded carvings were made for the room.

Of the smaller rooms in the house, the distinctly French-style Reception Room has notable wood paneling, which is ornamented with carved and gilded designs. It was taken from an old house in Paris, where it had been fashioned and installed by royal architects and carvers for the god-daughter of Queen Marie Antoinette. There is a neoclassical gilded Louis XVI (1774-93) suite of furniture upholstered in Beauvais tapestry and a Savonnerie rug.

On the second floor are ten less elaborate bedrooms, which were designed by Newport architect Ogden Codman. The woodwork and furniture are mostly painted antique ivory, and the walls are covered with figured fabric.

Each of the four elevations of the house is separately designed and has its own distinctive feature. Carvings in the Indiana limestone walls, terraces, and ballustrades are by Austrian-born sculptor Karl Bitter. Four large bronze candelabra flanking the entrance drive were made by Henri Bonnard of New York, after Italian models. An elegant wrought iron fence encloses three sides of the property. Single gates which flank the main drive gates were constructed from Italian designs by the William Jackson Company of New York.

The children's playhouse or "Cottage" exemplifies Victorian architecture on a small scale. Four wooden posts on the open porch are carved in the shape of figures from Dutch folklore. The large, open fireplace in the living room

contains seats within the opening. A built-in iron stove, sink, and china cupboard are seen in the kitchen.

The stables, located about one-half mile from The Breakers, contain a large carriage room, 26 open stalls, and two box stalls, in addition to harness, trophy, work, and office rooms. The stalls are "set fair," or properly dressed with neatly-arranged straw bedding and woven straw mats placed around the posts, as in the time they were actively used.

Surrounding The Breakers are parterre gardens, an ornamental garden area landscaped in a pattern. There are trees, including some unusual imported varieties, flowering shrubs, and spacious lawns.

Decatur House

Decatur House   748 Jackson Pl.   NW, Washington D.C. 20006   (202) 638-1204   Monday-Friday: 10-2; Saturday-Sunday: 12-4   Closed New Year's Day, Thanksgiving, and Christmas. Admission: adults $1.50; students and senior citizens 50¢.

Located across from the White House on Lafayette Square, the Decatur House was built in 1818 by Benjamin Henry Latrobe, one of the architects of the Capitol building, for Commodore Stephen Decatur, a naval war hero. It was a social and political center for more than 150 years; many statesmen, presidents, and other high government officials were either residents or guests here.

This unadorned, Federal-style, brick townhouse is a property of the National Trust for Historic Preservation. As was the custom of the day, the family living quarters and the master bedroom were on the first floor, drawing rooms on the second, and guest rooms on the third. The kitchen, stables, and servants' quarters were outbuildings.

Opposite: Banquet Hall at Biltmore House with acoustically perfect structure.

When the house was purchased in 1871 by Mary Edwards Beale, wife of General Edward Fitzgerald Beale, a major refurbishing in the romantic, Victorian style took place. Sandstone trim was added around the entrance and the first-floor windows, gaslights were installed, ceilings were frescoed with floral designs, and parquetry flooring was laid in the drawing room. While the first-floor furnishings have been returned to styles popular during Decatur's time, and include some of his original furniture and mementos, the second floor reflects the Victorian taste of the Beale family, who lived there from 1871 to 1956.

Of Decatur furnishings on the first floor, notable items include Stephen Decatur's drop-front mahogany desk, the bed in which he was born, and his portrait as a naval hero.

Furnishings on the second floor are a typically Victorian mixture from various periods. On display are Belter chairs (quality furniture manufactured by John H. Belter of New York in the mid-19th century, who worked with laminated wood in heavily-carved and curved frames with ornate floral designs). Also on view are 18th-century Philadelphia chairs, a Portuguese table, Chinese export porcelain, and 19th-century paintings.

Diplomatic Reception Rooms

The Diplomatic Reception Rooms of the United States Department of State   Washington D.C. 20520   (202) 632-3241   Three daily 45-minute tours are available.

One of the greatest collections of Americana in the United States is housed in the nine Diplomatic Reception Rooms atop the modern State Department building in Washington. Opened in 1961, the rooms are used, not only by the Secretary of State and State Department officials, but also by the President, Vice-President, Chief Justice,

and other Cabinet members for official entertainment, primarily of distinguished foreign visitors.

As backdrops to the furnishings and decorative arts, the rooms underwent architectural changes in order to give the appearance of an 18th-century house. Through the efforts of the Fine Arts Committee of the State Department, the rooms have been furnished by means of gifts and loans from private citizens, business establishments, and friends of the State Department. On display are some of the finest examples of American furniture, paintings, and decorative arts of the 18th and early 19th centuries.

The Entrance Hall, with its Georgian-style woodwork, contains fine furniture, American genre paintings, and decorative arts. Among principal items of interest is a Philadelphia highboy dating about 1775 and attributed to Joseph Deleveau. Also noteworthy is a Massachusetts secretary signed and dated 1753 by Benjamin Frothingham, the earliest documented piece of bombe furniture (a French style of furniture in which a chest, cabinet or commode swells outward and then recedes toward the bottom). There is a set of six mahogany Chippendale side chairs dating about 1775, which were once owned by Francis Scott Key, the author of the U.S. national anthem.

Also in the Entrance Hall is a rare collection of early Chinese export porcelain made for the American trade exhibited in an early English breakfront. The most popular decorations on the porcelain tableware, toiletware, and ornaments shown include the American eagle emblem and other patriotic motifs, ships flying the American flag, and floral motifs from Chinese gardens. In another breakfront are examples of early American silver and gold by famous 18th-century American silversmiths from Philadelphia, New York, Boston, and Delaware. Also on veiew is a rare musical tall clock built in 1776 by Benjamin Hanks, apprentice to Thomas Harland who started the clockmaking industry in Connecticut. Paintings by noted American artists Charles M. Russell, Edward Hicks, George Catlin, Frederic Remington, and Edwin Deakin are displayed.

The Gallery, which connects guests to the John Quincy Adams State Drawing Room, reveals mid-18th-century woodwork and Palladian windows. There are a Chippendale secretary-bookcase made in Boston about 1765, and a Goddard-Townsend three-shell blockfront chest of drawers from Newport of about 1765. One of the rarest pieces in the collecion is the Chippendale bombe chest of drawers made in Boston in 1765, one of seven existing chests of its kind. Also noteworthy is a Philadelphia Chippendale mahogany bonnet-top highboy with its matching lowboy. These two pieces, dating 1760-80, show a high development of the elaborate American rococo style of the third quarter of the 18th century.

Also in the Gallery from Philadelphia is a set of mahogany balloon-seat Queen Anne side chairs, formerly in the duPont Collection at Winterthur. Among Chinese export porcelain on display is a 65-piece set in the Fitzhugh pattern, characterized by a central medallion, floral panels, border of stylized butterflies, rectangular mosaics, the Greek fret, and flowering branches. There are oil paintings by American artists Granville Perkins, A.T. Bricher, and Maryland landscapist A. Weidenbach as well as antique Oriental rugs from Turkey and Persia which date around 1800.

In the Gentlemen's Lounge are several chairs of historical significance. One is a transitional mahogany Chippendale-Hepplewhite arm chair made in 1785, which was used at George Washington's Presidential inauguration in New York City. Others include Empire mahogany chairs designed by John Jay, Secretary for Foreign Affairs from 1784 to 1790, with the Jay family coat of arms carved on the back of each. There are several Philadelphia Chippendale chairs as well and a chest of drawers by William Savery, a Philadelphia cabinetmaker who worked in the ornamental Chippendale style.

Opposite: Mr. Vanderbilt's Bedroom at Biltmore House with Louis XIV furnishings.

The Ladies' Lounge, furnished predominantly in the Queen Anne style, contains a New York sofa in addition to tea tables from Massachusetts and Philadelphia. There are oil paintings by American artists R. Peale, James Henry Beard, William M. Harnett, John F. Kensett, and Eastman Johnson. A Khorasan rug dating around 1800 and a Chinese rug of about 1900 may also be seen.

The large and important John Quincy Adams State Drawing Room displays woodwork, wall paneling, and six period windows inspired by the notable Georgian architecture found in mid-18th-century Philadelphia houses. The predominantly Chippendale furnishings of the room are masterpieces of leading 18th-century American artists and cabinetmakers. One of the outstanding Chippendale case pieces is the mahogany secretary with bombe lower section that once belonged to the John Hancock family of Massachusetts. On the English Sheraton tambour desk with original brasses and leather, the Treaty of Paris of 1783, which ended the American Revolution, was signed. John Jay, a signatory, designed the Empire mahogany chair that stands before the desk.

In addition to Chinese export porcelains, many of which were used in prominent American homes, a superb collection of American 18th-century silver is also exhibited in the Adams Room. Works by Boston, New England, and New York silversmiths predominate and include such famous makers as Paul Revere I and II, Jeremiah Dummer, William Cowell, Benjamin Burt, Jacob Hurd, Simeon Soumain, Tobias Stoutenburgh, and Samuel Bartlett. Among notable artworks are the "Signing of the Treaty of Peace, Paris, 1782," an unfinished sketch by Benjamin West; oil portraits of John Jay and Robert R. Livingston by Gilbert Stuart; and oil portraits of George and Martha Washington by Rembrandt Peale dating about 1804. In the center of the room is an important 19th-century Lavehr Kerman Persian rug designed by Hassan Khan, which depicts the Persian nation's history from mythological times to the 19th-century in more than 300 large medallions.

The Thomas Jefferson State Reception Room reflects the late 18th-century Palladian style admired by Jefferson. The style is reflected in such details as the Doric entablature, pedimented niche with a life-sized statue of Jefferson, circular niches over the doorway containing busts of George Washington and John Paul Jones by noted French sculptor Jean Antoine Houdon, and marble mantel with caryatid supports. Museum-quality American Chippendale furnishings, including outstanding examples from Philadelphia, complete the ambience of the room. Among paintings by American artists on display are *View of Boston Harbor* by Fitz Hugh Lane, *New York Harbor* by Thomas Birch, *Henry Clay making His Great Speech* by John Neagle, and an oil portrait of John Marshall by Henry Inman.

Connected to the Jefferson Room by a Palladian arch, the Benjamin Franklin State Dining Room is used frequently with sideboards, mirrors, and paintings. on either side of the Palladian arch is a pair of American Chippendale looking glasses, called Constitution mirrors, with an American eagle displayed at the top of each. There are a Baltimore Hepplewhite sideboard of about 1780, a mahogany Federal sideboard by Duncan Phyfe, and a Sheraton mahogany and maple sideboard dating 1800-10. Notable works by European and American artists include a terra-cotta bust of Benjamin Franklin by Houdon and an oil portrait of Franklin by English artist Benjamin Wilson, who painted Franklin from life in 1758.

The suite of small reception rooms includes the James Monroe Reception Room, James Madison Dining Room, Martin Van Buren Dining Room, and Henry Clay Dining Room. The Monroe and Madison Rooms comprise a private suite of rooms for the Secretary of State's personal use in official functions where there is a small number of guests. They display furnishings of the period of these two Presidents. Particularly noteworthy are rare pieces with the American eagle design or inlay typical of the Federal period.

Master Bedroom at Glessner House (Chicago).

Parlor at Glessner House.

The Martin Van Buren Room is noteworthy for its display of fine art. On view are nine hand-colored engraved plates from the original elephant folio edition by Robert Havell, Jr. of London, 1828, entitled "Birds of America" by John James Audobon, America's foremost painter of wildlife. Also exhibited are works by American artists William Keith, Thomas Hill, Arthur Fitzwilliam Tait, Jane Stuart (daughter of famous American artist Gilbert Stuart), and Milton H. Lowell among other late 18th- and 19th-century painters.

The Clay Room contains a banjo clock by Simon Willard of Boston, dating about 1800-1810, among furnishings such as a New York mahogany highboy that once belonged to Philip Livingston, signer of the Declaration of Independence, and other pieces from Baltimore and Philadelphia.

The Reception Rooms and Offices of the Secretary of State, which are located on the seventh floor, are seen by visiting Chiefs of staff, Foreign Ministers, Ambassadors, and other high dignitaries. Furnishings include superb examples of Queen Anne, Chippendale, and Hepplewhite pieces from centers such as Philadelphia, Baltimore, and New York. There are also fine examples of Chinese export porcelain and silver on display. Paintings by established 20th-century American artists, such as Jack Tworkov, Victor Vasarely, and Jules Olitski, join 19th-century works by renown American artists such as John Singer Sargent, John Henry Twachtman, G.P.A. Healy, and Western genre painter Charles M. Russell.

Frick Collection

The Frick Collection   1 E. 70th St., New York, NY 10021   (212) 288-0700   Tuesday-Saturday: 10-6; Sunday: 1-6   June-August: closed Monday & Tuesday   Admission: Weekdays & Saturdays: $1:00; Sunday: $2.00; students & senior citizens: 50¢.

This outstanding collection is housed in the former residence of Henry Clay Frick, the Pittsburgh coke and steel industrialist. Built in 1913-14, it was designed by American architect Thomas Hastings in a style reminiscent of domestic European architecture of the 18th-century. The rooms are decorated in the style of English and French interiors of the same period. After certain alterations and additions were made to the residence, it was opened to the public in 1935. A further extension and a garden were completed in 1977.

During Frick's lifetime, the house contained the works of art he had collected over a period of 40 years. He bequeathed them to a board of trustees empowered to make the collection, along with his house, a center for the study of art and related subjects. Among the numerous works were 131 paintings. Since that time, some 40 additional paintings have been acquired by the trustees, mostly with funds from an endowment by Frick.

Interested in art from an early age, Frick began to collect French Salon and Barbizon school paintings. He purchased his first work by an old master around the turn of the century, and in the next decade acquired many more of the outstanding paintings that established the character of the collection on view today.

Works of art in the collection are arranged eclectically in furnished rooms to retain the atmosphere of a private home. The rooms have been turned into galleries and contain the finest examples of Italian Renaissance and 18th-century French furniture, as well as Italian bronzes and French and Chinese porcelains.

The Boucher Room exhibits the eight panels of the *Arts and Sciences* painted by Francois Boucher for Madame de Pompadour and some 18th-century French furniture. The Enamel Room is occupied by Piero della Francesca's *Saint Simon,* Duccio's *Temptation of Christ,* Jan van Eyck's

Guestroom at Glessner House. Wallpaper by William Morris (c. 1880).

Library at Glessner House.

Virgin and Child, and 16th-century painted enamels from Limoges.

Renaissance paintings in the collection feature works by Giovanni Bellini, Bronzino, Fra Filippo Lippi, Titian, and Veronese among others. French paintings include those of Jean-Baptiste Simeon-Chardin, Claude Lorrain, Camille Corot, Jacques-Louis David, Edgar Degas, Jean-Auguste Dominique Ingres, Charles-Francoise Daubigny, Edouard Manet, Jean-Francoise Millet, Claude Monet, and Pierre-Auguste Renoir. English paintings are also well represented and include works by John Constable, Thomas Gainsborough, William Hogarth, Sir Thomas Lawrence, Joseph M.W. Turner, Sir Joshua Reynolds, and George Romney. Dutch and Flemish paintings are represented by Pieter Breugel I, Sir Anthony van Dyck, Frans Hals, Meindert Hobbema, Rembrandt, Jan Vermeet, and others. Spanish painters include Francisco de Goya, Diego Velazquez, and El Greco. There are portraits by the American painters Gilbert Stuart and James A.M. Whistler, and well as the famous portrait *Sir Thomas More* by Hans Holbein the Younger.

From October until the end of May, illustrated lectures are given on Thursday, Friday, and Saturday afternoons. An introductory lecture is presented at 11:00 a.m. Tuesday through Friday during the lecture season. Chamber music concerts are also presented on Sundays fall through spring. A limited number of tickets are available by mail.

Getty Museum

J. Paul Getty Museum   17985 Pacific Coast Highway, Malibu, CA 90265
(213) 454-6541   Tuesday-Saturday (October-May): 10-5; Monday-Friday (June-September): 10-5   Admission free

Rococo Corner Cabinet (early 18th century) by Jacques DuBois. J. Paul Getty Museum.

The J. Paul Getty Museum is an 83,00-square foot structure situated in a ten-acre enclave on the 65-acre Getty ranch. It is located on Pacific Coast Highway one mile north of Sunset Boulevard and 4/5 mile south of Topanga Canyon Boulevard.

Established in 1953 in a Spanish-style home owned by J. Paul Getty, the museum housed an extensive art collection that Getty had started acquiring in the 1930s. Between 1953 and 1973 the original museum, which contained five galleries, averaged 250 visitors per week on a reservation-only basis. By the 1970s it could no longer accommodate Getty's vast collection. A new facility was built in a classical style to provide the proper backdrop for the entire collection of Greek and Roman antiquities.

The building is a recreation of the Villa dei Papiri (Villa of the Papyri), a luxurious Roman villa from the first century that stood on the slopes of Mount Vesuvius overlooking the Bay of Naples. The villa, which was buried when Mt. Vesuvius erupted in 79 A.D., was excavated in 1750. However, the project was abandoned, and today the villa remains underground. A floor plan and notes made during the excavation provided the basis for the museum building.

When Getty began acquiring art in the 1930s, he concentrated on Greek and Roman antiquities, Renaissance and baroque paintings, and 18th-century French decorative arts. Until his death, Getty approved or purchased every item in the collection.

Considered one of the finest of its kind in the United States, the collection of Greek and Roman antiquities contains ancient sculpture in bronze and marble, Greek vases, mosaics, frescoes, and ancient household items. Important pieces include the Lansdowne Herakles carved for the villa of the Emperor Hadrian, and the Mazarin Venus. Two noteworthy groups are fourth-century Attic stelai (funerary monuments) and Greek and Roman portraits.

Living Hall at Glessner House.

Tea Room at Monticello.

Major schools of Western art from the 13th through the early 20th centuries are well represented in the collection of paintings. The museum's focus, however, is on the Renaissance and baroque art, spanning the 15th to the 18th centuries. Getty's original collection consisted mainly of Italian paintings of the 16th century and Netherlandish works from the 17th century. Included in the present expanded collection are works by Masaccio, Peter Paul Rubens, Georges de la Tour, Thomas Gainsborough, Rembrandt, Giovanni Lanfranco, and Francois Boucher.

The collection of decorative arts includes furniture, carpets, tapestries, clocks, chandeliers, and small decorative items made for the French nobility and royal household from the early years of the reign of Louis XIV to the French Revolution (1670-1790). The quality of the collection is considered to be comparable to holdings in the Metropolitan Museum and the Frick Collection in New York. Many of the objects are displayed in paneled period rooms.

The museum's impressive, serene gardens include trees, flowers, shrubs, and herbs that might have been growing 2000 years ago at the Villa dei Papiri. The landscape, pathways, and resting areas reflect Roman fascination with geometric design. Boxwood, which was used extensively in Roman gardens, is featured in the Main Peristyle Garden.

The museum's herb garden reflects the same manicured, geometric landscape as the formal pleasure gardens. It was designed on the basis that every Roman villa had allotted a section of land for an herb and kitchen garden to provide fresh fruits, vegetables, and herbs. The bronze statues in the gardens are modern castings of ones unearthed during the 18th-century excavations of the villa; the originals are on display in the Naples Museum.

The research library concentrates on the three major areas represented in the museum. It is used for documentation of art historical items in the museum, preparation of catalogs and other museum publications, selection and documentation of acquisitions, and other scholarly research. Used primarily by the museum staff, the library is open to those involved in specialized research. There are presently about 20,000 sales catalogs and 20,000 volumes.

Glessner House

John Jacob Glessner House   1800 S. Prairie Ave.   Chicago, IL 60616
(312) 326-1393   Tuesday, Thursday, and Saturday: 10-4; Sunday: 1-5

Built in 1886, Glessner House is the only building designed by American architect Henry Hobson Richardson to have survived in Chicago. This Prairie Avenue house is widely acknowledged to be his masterpiece of residential design.

Richardson, who introduced the Romanesque revival style in architecture, designed the solid and heavy-looking, rock-faced granite house in the basic form of a medieval manor. The detail, especially the rounded-arched doorway, is an abstraction from architecture of the 11th and 12th-century Romanesque period. The inner side of the house is open to lawns and gardens, a Victorian treatment that became basic to modern architecture.

Now owned by the Chicago School of Architecture Foundation, the house contains much of the original Glessner furniture. The Living Hall, Dining Room, School Room, Library, Parlor, Master Bedroom, and other rooms in this large house display antique furniture and decorative household items by a number of leading designers and artisans of the period. Most were practitioners of the arts and crafts movement (also called gothic revival, American colonial revival, reform or aesthetic movement). This was an attitude that embraced

Assembly Room at Hearst Castle. (San Simeon, CA.)

Main Library at Hearst Castle.

simplicity, elimination of excessive ornamentation, and respect for materials, as well as an interest in the aesthetic importance of both fine art works and objects for everyday use.

Furniture by Richardson was designed in conjunction with the mood and details of the architectural elements of a room. The Glessner House dining room chairs of 1887, adapted from American Windsor chairs, betray their sources in the American colonial revival, also reflected in the character of the room. Completed after Richardson's death, the chairs are attributed to designer Charles A. Coolidge, head draftsman in Richardson's office at the time of his death, and were manufactured by A.H. Davenport and Co., Boston furniture makers.

Glessner House furnishings by Isaac E. Scott, one of the most important 19th-century designer-craftsmen in Chicago, reflect the reform movement in the decorative arts and a first-hand familiarity with English furniture of the period. The bookcase of 1875 in the Upper Hallway is recognized as a masterpiece of modern gothic furniture. Other Scott designs in the house include a bed and matching mirrored bureau, and tall chest of drawers or press cabinet, both of the late 1870s and on display in the Master Bedroom. Scott also designed picture frames for the Glessner print collection, featuring Dutch and German works of the 15th through the 17th centuries; as well as ceramic vases, which reveal the influence of Japanese taste prevalent in American decorative arts at that time.

Opposite: Neptune Pool at Hearst Castle.

Furniture by the Hester Brothers of New York is also represented in Glessner House, notably two ebonized chairs in the Parlor. These furniture makers were among the first American firms to import oriental decorative arts (Chinese porcelains, Persian pottery and embroideries, and Japanese objects) and to use oriental motifs and ebonizing technique in their interiors and furniture and wallpaper designs, following the appearance of Japanese goods at Chicago's Centennial Exposition of 1889. The understatment and restraint of Japanese art appealed to many proponents of the arts and crafts movement. Among Japanese objects owned by the Glessners, a large 19th-century jar of folk pottery from southern Japan is placed near the School Room.

William Morris, poet and pre-Raphaelite painter who shifted his interest to utilitarian domestic architecture and interior decoration, designed almost everything from fabrics and wallpaper to books and furniture. His wallpaper designs, known for their pattern, movement, and use of naturalistic elements, can be seen in various rooms of the house. Textiles on view include draperies, upholstery, and tapestries.

William de Morgan's ceramic Persian-ware tiles are located in the Master Bedroom. Other extant de Morgan-designed decorated tiles owned by the Glessners are found on the floors of the kitchen areas and vestibule. They are encaustic tiles (with burnt-in colored ornamentation) produced in the English Minton factory, famous for its high-quality Spode-like creamware. Ceramic tiles, mostly mass-produced, became popular in the last decades of the 19th century.

Governor's Palace at Colonial Williamsburg

The Governor's Palace at Colonial Williamsburg   Palace Green, Williamsburg, VA 23185   Colonial Williamsburg Foundation Information Office (804) 229-1000   Admission by reservation only.   Admission fee.

The Governor's Palace is one of more than 80 period homes, shops, and public buildings and nearly 100 gardens that comprise the restored capital of Colonial Virginia. All of Colonial Williamsburg has been listed on the National Register

of Historic Places and declared a National Historic Landmark.

The Palace served as the official residence of seven royal governors and the first two elected governors of the Virginia Commonwealth, Patrick Henry and Thomas Jefferson. Designed by Virginia governor Alexander Spotswood in 1706, completed 14 years later, and extended in 1750-51, it consisted of a central building with numerous outbuildings. The Palace was destroyed by fire in 1781, reconstructed between 1931 and 1934, and refurnished in 1981.

The ample and elegant central mansion of the Governor's Palace is one of the finest examples in America of the classic Queen Anne house, derived from the designs of English architect Sir Christopher Wren. It combines the blocky form and hipped roof of the Italian Palladian villa with the red brick of a traditional English dwelling, also typical of other Virginia Tidewater mansions.

The recent refurnishing was meticulously based on the inventory of the penultimate royal governor, Lord Botetourt, which dates 1700. It itemizes more than 16,500 objects contained in the 61 rooms of the Palace complex. As one of the most authentically furnished historic buildings of the pre-Revolutionary War period, the Palace features 18th-century furnishings. In addition to large sets of items such as tables, chairs, dressers, chests, and other pieces both imported and local, the furnishings include some of the finest examples of colonial upholstery, bed coverings, and carpets; muskets, pistols, and swords; dining and lighting accoutrements of silver, cut glass, porcelain, and brass; prints and maps; and paintings.

The Ballroom, which served as a setting for large dinner parties as well as dances, contains eight candelabra on brackets, numerous mahogany chairs, four large dining tables, and a large carpet. The room is decorated with blue paper bordered with a strip of gilt-enbossed leather, one of the earliest instances of the neoclassic aesthetic in the Colonies. In addition to glass chandeliers, there are large portraits of George III and Queen Charlotte by Allan Ramsay, which Lord Botetourt brought with him from England when he came to be governor of Virginia in 1768.

The Dining Room contains an extensive display of silver as well as examples of early Chelsea porcelain. In addition to Chelsea, a large amount of Staffordshire and Worcester pieces, both useful and ornamental, may be seen elsewhere in the Palace.

Hearst Castle

Hearst Castle   P.O. Box 8, San Simeon, CA 93452   (805) 927-4621   Daily, except New Year's Day, Thanksgiving, and Christmas. Visitor Center opens 8 a.m. Advance ticket reservations are required for all tours.

Hearst Castle, called La Cuesta Encantada (The Enchanted Hill), is a villa commissioned by the wealthy publisher William Randolph Hearst and designed beginning in 1919 by Berkeley architect Julia Morgan. The Castle stands on a hill five miles from and 160 feet above the Pacific Ocean, encompassed by about 75,000 of originally 250,000 acres of property Hearst had inherited from his parents.

Opposite: Facade—La Cava Grande—at Hearst Castle.

The Castle consists of five main buildings: the Hispano-Moresque-style main house, La Casa Grande; three Mediterranean-Renaissance-style guest houses, Casa del Mar, Casa del Monte, and Casa del Sol; and a neoclassical-style gymnasium unit. The vast Hearst art collection is displayed as an intrinsic part of the architecture, interior decoration, and surrounding grounds of the Castle. The collection on view possibly represents one-tenth of Hearst's entire holdings, which he acquired from 1894 to the mid-1940s. The collection is eclectic; a rich diversity of art forms of different media, styles, periods, and places exists in nearly every interior room as well as outside the buildings.

The most unique part of the Hearst collection is the group of ceilings of the

Castle proper and the guest houses. Almost every ceiling of La Casa Grande is an antique from Spain or Italy. Most of the painted ceilings are from medieval or Renaissance Spain, and some contain elements of Moorish geometric design. In Hearst's private bedroom is a rare 14th-century ceiling from Teuruel, Spain, with 53 panels, each painted with a figure of a saint. In the South Lower Duplex, another notable ceiling incorporates oil-on-canvas paintings by the 18th-century French painter Jean-Baptiste Van Loo.

The furniture in the Castle constitutes a rich collection of broad range and variety. Chairs extend from beautifully carved European choir stalls to nondescript, overstuffed seats that were typical of the period during which the castle was furnished. In the Refectory, a set of 22 Italian Renaissance Dante chairs (X-shaped chairs whose legs become the arms) are characterized by their "velvet of the Doges" design (with seats and backs of leather covered with Italian velvet). A 16th-century Savonarola folding chair is found in the Library.

Also on view are chairs with tapestry seats, such as two French Renaissance armchairs in the New Wing, called *caquetoire,* which were used by women for chatting. Also in the New Wing is a setee and five 18th-century French chairs from the Regency period, with gilt frames and needlepoint covers.

Other furniture includes outstanding examples of papeleras, varguenos, credenzas, trunks, cassoni, and tables. Papeleras (Moorish chests with a large number of drawers and cupboards) can be found in several rooms and hallways. Credenzas (sideboards, originally used in the 15th, 16th, and 17th centuries for testing food) are found in the Library and the New Wing.

Marriage chests and leather or wood trunks are among several types of chests and trunks found at the Castle. A painted and hinged 15th-century Gothic marriage chest fitted inside with drawers and trays is found in the Casa del Sol. Other furniture includes beds, bedside tables, stools, prayer benches, cabinets, and framed mirrors.

Both classical and neoclassical sculpture is well represented at Hearst Castle. Classical pieces (original work produced in ancient Greece and Rome), are usually marble or bronze copies and are placed both inside and outside the Castle. Neoclassical pieces (18th- and 19th-century sculpture inspired by classical work) can be found in the interior rooms. Roman sarcophagi made of limestone are scattered throughout the garden. Notable neoclassical works by 19th-century artists are a copy of *The Three Graces* originally by Antonio Canova, several pieces by French artist Jean Leon Gerome, and a statue of Venus by Danish sculptor Bertel Thorvaldsen, who is also represented by four medallions in the Assembly Room. Other important sculpture in the Castle includes works by the famous Della Robbia family of Renaissance Italy.

Displayed throughout the Castle are numerous ceramic vases from ancient Greece, China, and Persia. Though part of the Hearst Greek vase collection was given to the Metropolitan museum upon his death, what remains is still one of the largest private holdings. Greek vases are found in the Library and represent a variety of shapes, including amphorae, hydrias, kraters, pithos, rhytons, alabastrans, and askos. A 12th-century pitcher from Sultanabad, Persia is displayed in Hearst's private bedroom and Italian Majolica pieces are found in several other rooms of the Castle.

The painting collection, which includes Italian, French, Spanish, German, Flemish, and Dutch paintings, features 13th- and 14th-century Italian works. The relief *The Madonna and Child and St. John* by Duccio, a major central Italian figure of the early Renaissance, is located in the Doge's Suite, as is the portrait *Bianca Capello, Duchess of Medici* by 16th-century Florentine

Roman Pool at Hearst Castle.

Refectory at Hearst Castle.

painters Angelo Allori (Il Bronzino). Displayed in the Casa del Sol is a pair of portraits by Bartolome Gonzales, a 16th-century Spanish court painter.

The silver pieces on view at the Castle are a sample of a much larger collection. Much of the silver is found in the Refectory, which contains, among other silver items, an Irish mace from Dublin, an enormous wine cistern from England, candlesticks from France and Spain, a Spanish processional banner, and an assortment of covered dishes from England and Ireland. A tall silver lamp made by Tiffany & Co., New York, is the most visible item in the room.

Objects carved in jade, rock crystal or glass are scattered throughout the Castle. A 16th-century rock crystal presentation case is placed on an Italian Renaissance table in the Assembly Room. French artisan Rene Lalique, whose work spans the art nouveau period of the 1890s and the art deco period of the 1920s and 1930s, is represented by a number of objects at the Castle.

The superior tapestry collection is characterized by a great diversity of style and technique. Four matching tapestries designed in the Mannerist style by 16th-century Italian artist Guilio Romano are hung in the Assembly Room. In the same room is a baroque tapestry by Peter Paul Rubens, which was woven in Brussels about 1625. A *mille-fleur* French tapestry of the late 15th or early 16th century, which is the focal point of the Billiards Room, depicts a stag hunt in progress. An 18th-century royal Persian silk rug from Turiz and a rare 17th-century Spanish tapestry decorated with a coat of arms are in the New Wing.

Most of the rooms in the Castle contain oriental rugs representing many famous rug-making areas of Turkey and Iran. However, nearly all are partly covered with tour mats and furniture and are therefore difficult to appreciate.

Lyndhurst

Lyndhurst   635 Broadway (U.S. Route 9) Tarrytown, NY 10591
May-October: Tuesday-Sunday, 10-5; November-April: Tuesday-Sunday, 10-4   Closed holidays.   Admission: $3.00

Perched on a promontory overlooking the Hudson River, Lyndhurst evokes all the grandeur of the Gilded Age and represents the culmination of gothic revival architecture during this period of romanticism in America. The estate was shaped over 140 years by three families, the Pauldings, the Merritts, and the Goulds.

Lyndhurst was designed in 1838 by Alexander Jackson Davis, one of the most enthusiastic exponents of gothic revival architecture in America. It was enlarged from a country villa into a mansion in 1865. On the exterior, the house is characterized by an asymmetrical array of peaks, pinnacles, turrets, and porches. Inside, the gothic mood dominates, with its ribbed and vaulted ceilings, pointed arches, stained glass windows, and heavy gothic furnishings. The furnishings and decorations of the mansion reflect the lifestyles of the three families: the Pauldings' early gothic style, the Merritts' high (flamboyant) Victorian gothic style, and the Goulds' French 18th-century revival style and Beaux-Arts style (based mostly on French decorative art of the Renaissance).

The reception room contains the only mantelpiece of the house that still retains its original gothic overmantel mirror. The ceiling, copied from Renaissance artist Raphael's *Hours*, was painted directly on the plaster. Renaissance revival upholstered furniture is also seen in this room.

In the art gallery/billard room, the exposed roof beams end in corbels of cast heads, which represent Washington, Franklin, Shakespeare, Milton, and Dante. Furnishings in this room designed by Davis include a gothic table and two types of gothic chairs.

Opposite: Monticello Dining Room.

The dining room features a gothic mantelpiece and gothic furniture. The walls of painted plaster with a gold raised stencil design have been carefully restored. Simulated marble woodwork, a popular craft in the 19th century, imitates the three kinds of marble in the mantelpiece.

In the state bedroom, used as the principal guest room from 1840 to 1940, there is a beautiful gothic bed, which may have been designed by Davis. The ceiling has a richly-colored design probably painted in 1865, and there is a painted border around the base of the room.

The grounds at Lyndhurst are important examples of 19th-century landscape architecture and complement the picturesque mansion. The building program included one of the largest private greenhouses ever constructed, kennels, a recreation building, a children's playhouse, and a formal rose garden.

Lyndhurst was designated a National Historic Landmark in 1966 and is now operated by the National Trust for Historic Preservation as a historic house museum. It is also the setting for concerts, lectures, special events, and horticultural programs. From its Restoration Workshop at Lyndhurst, the National Trust provides on-site restoration work for its own properties as well as those of other preservation organizations.

Monticello

Monticello   State Route 52, P.O. Box 316, Charlottesville, VA 22902   (804) 293-2158   March-October: daily 8-5; November-February: daily 9-4:30   Admission: adults $3; children 6-11 $1

Monticello is the home of President Thomas Jefferson, who was the architect of his own hilltop estate. Between 1769 and 1809, Jefferson was constantly involved with the construction and enlargement of Monticello, which uses elements of Roman, Palladian, and 18th-century French styles.

Opposite: Monticello, home of Thomas Jefferson (Charlottesville, VA.)

Turning to Republican Rome for inspiration, Jefferson designed his brick-and-frame mansion in the Palladian style (influenced by the designs of 16th-century Italian architect Palladio, who worked in the classical style). Jefferson's inventive contributions that can be seen include a dumbwaiter incorporated into the dining-room mantle which facilitated serving meals to the family's guests, beds that disappear into walls, built-in closets, and folding doors.

The Entrance Hall contains many items from Jefferson's museum, one of the most important private collections of natural history specimens and American Indian artifacts in America during his lifetime. In addition, there is a seven-day calendar clock run by cannon-ball-like weights. Windsor chairs are found among the few furnishings of this room.

In all rooms of the house, the furnishings, with few exceptions, belonged to Jefferson or his family. Of particular interest in Jefferson's Bedroom are a blockfront bureau table and a two-drawer worktable made at Monticello. Opposite the bedroom, Jefferson's Cabinet, a study, contains a revolving chair, Windsor couch, table, and telescope. Connected to the Cabinet, the Library houses duplicates of his original books in bindings not later than 1826. The room is furnished with a reading table from Virginia, an American octagonal filing table, and a camera obscura, a box-like optical device that preceded the camera. Adjacent to the Library is the South Square Room, used as a sitting room, which has a portrait of Martha Jefferson Randolph, Jefferson's eldest daughter when she was 64, painted by English-born Thomas Sully.

The Parlor has a parquet floor—one of the earliest of its kind in America—which follows Jefferson's design. Many of the furnishings reflect his purchases in Paris between 1784 and 1789, such as French mahogany armchairs and a brass-bound marble table top. In the Dining Room, many pieces of Jefferson's silver are visible in the

butler's secretary. The mantle of the fireplace incorporates Wedgewood plaques. The Tea Room displays a table and chairs made in Williamsburg, probably by Peter Scott. The North Octagonal Room, or "Madison" Room, is presently the only room in the house with wallpaper, whose pattern reproduces one that Jefferson obtained in Paris.

The second and third floors are not open to visitors. The second floor has rooms used as emergency sleeping quarters and for storage, and the third floor contains three bedrooms with skylights.

Balustraded terraces extend from the house to small pavillions at the ends of a "U"-shaped configuration. They shelter the dependency structures, namely the smokeroom, dairy, servants' quarters, and kitchen on one side, and the stables, coach house, and the ice house on the other side. These are accessible by the underground passages.

Among the outbuildings still standing on the estate is the first guest house Jefferson built in 1770. The gardens and walks are restored according to Jefferson's surviving plans. The gardens are planted with many of the original species of flowers laid out in the later years of his presidency. A grove, vegetable garden, and orchard have also been restored. Nearby is the family cemetery, where Jefferson is buried.

Morris-Jumel Mansion

The Morris-Jumel Mansion   W. 160th St. & Edgecombe Ave., New York, NY 10032   (212) 923-8008   Tuesday-Sunday: 10-4   Closed New Year's Day, Thanksgiving, and Christmas.   Admission fee charged.   Reservations are required for all group tours. Special arrangements are made for guided tours.

Opposite: Parlor at Monticello. Cherry & beechwood parquet floors designed by Thomas Jefferson; believed to be first of its kind in America.

Situated among apartment houses and brownstones in upper Manhattan, this beautiful Georgian mansion is the oldest private dwelling extant on the Island. Listed in the National Register of Historic Places, it is a New York City landmark. Surrounding the mansion is Roger Morris Park with its rose and colonial-style herb gardens, paths, and bench-lined areas.

The mansion originally was the summer residence of Colonel Roger Morris and his family. During the American Revolution, the house and its estate, Mount Morris, once served as General George Washington's headquarters. In 1810, French wine merchant Stephen Jumel bought and restored the house and its property. After the death of its last private owner, General Ferdinand P. Earle, the house and some of its property were purchased by the City of New York in 1903 to preserve the mansion as an architectural structure and a historic museum.

Inside the mansion, the drawing room displays hand-painted Chinese wallpaper and English furniture, reflecting the Morrises' taste. In the front parlor, where the wallpaper is a copy of the original imported from Paris by Madame Jumel, several original Jumel pieces of furniture are exhibited. Madame Jumel's bedroom contains objects acquired from Napoleon Bonaparte's family and furnishings of the Empire period (a predominantly neoclassical style popular in America from 1810 to 1840 and characterized by massive forms which were lavishly trimmed). Objects once belonging to Colonel Aaron Burr, former Vice-President of the United States who was briefly married to Madame Jumel in 1833 after her husband died, are displayed in his bedroom. A portion of the basement kitchen has been restored to show cooking methods used by the Morris staff.

Programs for children, workshops, lectures, concerts, and special observances of patriotic events are frequently presented throughout the year.

Mount Vernon

Mount Vernon   George Washington Memorial Parkway, Mount Vernon Ladies' Association, Mount Vernon, VA 22121   (703) 780-2000   March-October: daily 9-5 November-February: daily 9-4   Admission: $3.00 adults, $2.50 senior citizens; $1.00 children 6-11 and students; free September-February

Overlooking the Potomac River near Washington D.C., Mount Vernon was the plantation home and final resting place of President George Washington. In 1754, Washington came into possession of the house, which was built in 1743, and developed Mount Vernon into one of the finest estates of the period. Besides enlarging the main house, he built a complex of outbuildings and landscaped the grounds.

Mount Vernon, a Palladian Georgian, classical-revival building, is noted for its full-length, two-story portico facing the river as well as its well-integrated service buildings. The outbuildings, gardens, and grounds remain as Washington designed them. Within the mansion, 14 rooms display numerous original furnishings that have been returned to Mount Vernon since the Mount Vernon Ladies' Association purchased the estate in 1858.

The Large Dining Room or New Room, with its stately Palladian window on the north wall, contains an English carved-marble mantel and English mantel vases of Worcester porcelain, signed by Jeffrey Hamet O'Neale. Notable furnishings of the room include a pair of neoclassic Hepplewhite sideboards, one of which was made in 1797 by John Aitken of Philadelphia. A row of chairs by Aitken, originally 24 in number, is also on display. Large works in oil by 18th-century landscape painters George Beck and William Winstanley are on view.

A feature of the Little Parlor or Common Parlor is the harpsichord that Washington imported from London in 1793 for Mrs. Washington's granddaughter Nelly Curtis Lewis. In addition to prints of marine scenes, there is a rare trio of small mezzotint portraits of Washington, Benjamin Franklin, and George Washington Lafayette. The Windsor chairs in the room were made by Robert Gaw, brother of the Philadelphia chairmaker who made Windsor chairs for Washington.

The West Parlor, which probably dates from the first enlargement of the house, is one of the finest surviving examples of colonial Virginia interior design. A carved and painted representation of the Washington family coat of arms hangs in the pediment over the mantel. An original mirror, also displaying the coat of arms, is on view. American painter Charles Willson Peale is represented in the room by the portrait of Washington which he painted during the Revolution. Among original portraits are companion pastels of the General and Mrs. Washington by James Sharples. Other original items include silver lamps, a silver tray and hot water urn, a china tea set, and a Chippendale card table.

On display in the Small Dining Room are many pictures, including an engraved portrait of the Washington family. There are Chippendale ladder-back chairs, a mahogany dining table, and an English sideboard table.

On the second floor of the mansion are five bedrooms in addition to the master's sleeping quarters. The walls of some of the rooms were originally papered, although the original designs have not survived. Reproductions of period designs may be seen. One bedroom contains the trunk that accompanied Mrs. Washington on her trips to and from the quarters of the American Army during the Revolution. In Washington's bedroom are leather fire buckets from Philadelphia which bear his name.

The bedroom of George and Martha Washington contains their original bed, which was made in Philadelphia. Washington's "shaving and dressing table" and Mrs. Washington's writing desk are French. Other items in the room constitute Mount Vernon memorabilia, such as a knee-hole dressing table and lacquered dressing glass, prints in original round frames, and portraits of Washington family members by Robert Edge Pine.

Opposite: Mr. Phipps', Study at Westbury House (Old Westbury, NY).

The Study or Library was Washington's headquarters, an important room from which he directed the management of his estate. It contains Washington's original French dressing table and secretary-desk. Also one of the original furnishings of the room, the terrestrial globe was made in London. Other Washington memorabilia include a whip stock, large ducking gun, gold-headed walking staff, and iron chest in which the President kept important papers. Although most of the Library's original 884 volumes have been dispersed, over 75 of these have been acquired and over 300 of the remaining titles are represented by duplicates of the same imprints and grouped in the room as they were listed by the executors.

In the Pantry, over 100 pieces of blue-and-white Canton china that correspond to the original ware used by the Washington family are on display. Original Mount Vernon pieces to be found are a large wine chest imported from London and a pine serving table with serpentine front.

Of the courtyard dependencies, the kitchen contains various utensils of the period, although few of the original pieces have survived. The original items on display include a large iron mortar, pewter plates with hot water compartments, a trivet, an iron stand, and a metal skillet.

The Museum, a modern structure, was erected in 1928 to house the Mount Vernon's Ladies' Association's growing collection of memorabilia. One of the most valuable holdings is a Washington bust modeled at Mount Vernon by celebrated French 18th-century sculptor Jean Antoine Houdon. The collection includes military items, books and documents, domestic china and silver, textiles and articles of clothing, and portraits. Occasionally there are displays of memorabilia, documents or pictures relating to special themes, which are held in a wing of the reconstructed greenhouse.

The subsidiary buildings, which housed many people and served a variety of essential purposes, are harmoniously incorporated with the mansion. The spinning house displays reels, spinning wheels, and other implements representative of the equipment originally used there. In addition, the smokehouse, washhouse, and coachhouse are among about a dozen dependencies open to public view. The coach compartment of the stable houses a coach in use at the time of Washington's death, and the coachhouse contains a chaise, or two-wheeled riding chair, one belonging to Washington's friend and patron Lord Thomas Fairfax.

Old Merchants House

Old Merchants House   29 E. 4th St., New York, NY 10003 (212) 777-1089
Sunday: 1-4   Closed August.   Admission: $2.00 adults, $1.00 students and senior citizens.

A New York landmark, the Old Merchants House is located in the middle of warehouses and parking lots bordering on the Bowery, a street named after the Dutch word for plantation. Built in 1832, it is the only 19th-century house in Manhattan to survive intact with its original furniture and family memorabilia and in a remarkable state of preservation.

The house was constructed by a hat manufacturer turned real estate speculator, Joseph Brewster, as one of a row of luxury dwellings on a newly fashionable block. It was bought in 1835 by Seabury Tredwell, a prosperous hardware merchant and descendant of Samuel Seabury, the first bishop of the Episcopal Church in New York. For nearly 100 years the Tredwell family inhabited the house until Gertrude, the last of eight Tredwell children, died in 1933. The house has undergone careful restoration from the 1970s.

Built during the peak of the Greek revival style in America, the brick house presents a classical facade wih its columned door surmounted by an ornately

Upper Hall at Old Westbury House (Old Westbury, NY).

West Porch at Old Westbury House.

carved fanlight and quoined marble arch. On the formal reception floor, the double parlor displays a pair of late Greek revival pier tables (side tables used in conjunction with a pier mirror designed to fill a window pier). There are also more profusely decorated Rococo revival pier mirrors which Eliza Tredwell installed during her redecoration of the house after her husband's death in 1865.

Among noteworthy architectural elements in the double parlor are two black marble fireplaces and matching chandeliers—the original whale oil fixtures later converted to gas and then electricity, as well as paired portraits of Seabury and Eliza Tredwell. The two parlors can be completely divided in the center of the house by hidden sliding doors which are veneered in grained mahogany and ornamented with silver handles. The front room was always a formal parlor; the back chamber was converted from a second parlor into a formal dining room in 1865.

The parlor furniture is a mixture of Greek revival and later pieces. It is likely that some of the fine unlabeled pieces were made by one of the prominent 19th-century New York cabinet makers, such as Michael Allison or Joseph Meeks.

Under the parlor rooms is the first floor containing the kitchen, pantry, and original family dining room. The kitchen displays a brick fireplace, original Dutch oven, and hand pump connected to the 4,000-gallon cistern in the rear garden. On the floor above the parlors are a small study, which contains a Gothic revival secretary, and two large bedrooms. Each bedroom features a monumental Greek revival bed embellished with different carved and gilded canopy decorations. There are also closets filled with dresses, gloves, parasols, bonnets, shoes, shawls, and books.

Smith Museum

Abigail Adams Smith Museum   421 E. 61st., New York, NY 10021   (212) 838-6878   Monday-Friday: 10-4   Closed August and major holidays. Admission fee charged; children under 12 free.   Guided tours are available. Research facilities are available to scholars by appointment.

Opposite: Dining Nook at Abigail Adams Smith House (New York).

This Federal-style stone building was constructed in 1799 as a carriage house to complement a manor house on property previously owned by Colonel William Smith and his wife Abigail Adams, daughter of President John Adams. Colonel Smith had served under George Washington during the American Revolution and named the estate "Mount Vernon" in honor of Washington's Virginia home. Due to the Smith's financial dificulties, the estate was sold to William T. Robinson, a New York merchant who prospered in the China trade. It became one of a number of fashionable country estates that lined the east River in the early 19th century. After being used as a private residence for several years, the mansion became the Mount Vernon Hotel in the 1820s and later a female academy, burning to the ground in 1826.

The coachhouse, constructed of Manhattan schist, was remodeled as an inn by Joseph Hart. The arched openings for horses and carriages were filled in with brick, two porticos were added to the exterior, and the open interior was divided into smaller rooms. The mantels, plaster cornices, and details of the stair added at this time were Greek revival in style.

The property was sold in 1833 to Jeremiah Towle, one of the first commissioners of Central Park, and his family lived in the stone building for three generations. In 1903 the house and grounds were bought by the Standard Gas and Light Company. In 1919, the house was leased to open a shop for antiques and colonial crafts. Here the president of The Society of American Antiquarians trained neighborhood women to spin and weave wool on the

premises; the fabrics were sold exclusively to Abercrombie and Fitch.

The Colonial Dames of America, who purchased the building in 1924, restored the house, planted an 18th-century garden around it, and assembled a collection of furniture and artifacts of the Federal style (1790-1820). These furnishings are displayed in nine period rooms, which have been open to the public since 1939.

On the first floor in the dining room are American Sheraton chairs that belonged to Abigail Adams Smith. Sheraton furniture was based on the designs of Thomas Sheraton in London between 1790 and 1805, and is characterized by straight lines and gentle curves with light, elegant forms. The music room has a harp, piano, and barrel organ. In the kitchen are two tin reflector ovens and a brass bed warmer.

On the second floor the visitor will find a wooden cradle, handmade toys, a dress made and worn by Abigail Adams Smith, whale oil lamps, John Adam's Presidential Seal, letters from Adams in addition to James Monroe and George Washington, and more Federal-style furniture. Each room is completely furnished, from wallpaper and rugs to candlesticks and birdcages.

Tryon Palace

Tryon Palace   610 Pollock St., P.O. Box 1007, New Bern, NC 28560   (919) 638-5109   Tuesday-Saturday: 9:30-4; Sunday: 1:30-4   Open Monday only on Easter, Memorial Day, and Labor Day. Closed New Year's Day, Thanksgiving, and December 24-26.   Admission fee charged; reduced admission for students.   Reservations are required for tour groups of 15 or more persons.

Located in New Bern, North Carolina's second oldest town, Tryon Palace itself was both the capitol building and royal residence of North Carolina's governor from 1770 until the American Revolution. This 38-room mansion is the central building of a 13-acre formal garden complex which contains other historical landmarks. Among these are two notable homes, the John Wright Stanley House (1780s), Georgian mansion with high-style 18th-century furniture; and the Stevenson House (c. 1805), a Federal-style townhouse furnished with Federal and Empire antiques.

Completed in 1770, Tryon Palace was built by Royal Governor William Tryon and designed by English architect John Hawks. It was destroyed by fire in 1798, but restored and reconstructed in the 1950s. It is furnished with authentic 18th-century English and American antiques.

The Council chamber displays full-length portraits of King George III and his consort, Queen Charlotte, by the school of Sir Joshua Reynolds; a pair of looking glasses made about 1720 by English cabinetmaker and glass manufacturer John Gumley; an Isfahan rug once in the Braganza palace in Portugal; and the Governor's writing desk, formerly in Lulworth Castle, England. In addition, there is a pair of Council tables made by the famous Goddard-Townsends of Newport, Rhode Island; twelve square Gothic-Chippendale chairs; a large, musical, mechanical clock made about 1736; and 18th-century cut-glass chandeliers.

In the dining room, the floor supports a Turkish hand-tufted carpet of about 1770 in an English strapwork (ornamental scroll motif) design. There are a Chippendale mahogany dining table and Chippendale tall-case (grandfather) clock with a dial worked in silver by James Warne of London.

The Palace parlor, which was used variously as a music room, ballroom, living room or senate chamber, contains a 16th-century Turkish carpet, a walnut spinet made by Thomas Hitchcock, and a breakfront from a design of Thomas Chippendale. There is also a suite of seven George II mahogany chairs

Main Building and Wings, Tryon Palace (New Bern, N.C.)

Harpsichord at Tryon Palace.

and a card table by William Vile, who was prominent among the cabinet makers to the royal household of George III.

The library holds first editions of 400 of the same books owned by the Tryons. In this room there is a Thomas Gainsborough portrait of Philip Bowes Broke dating about 1755, and a carved mahogany kneehold desk (a desk with a central cutout for legs, with sides of drawers or panels) with a roundabout chair.

Upstairs at Tryon Palace are the bedrooms and dressing rooms, and a family supper room and a drawing room. In the Governor's bedroom is a hand-tufted English Wilton carpet of about 1750 with an oriental design. Also displayed are a carved canopy bed, a Queen Anne bonnet-top highboy (high chest of drawers) in burled walnut made in Massachusetts around 1730-40, and a mahogany kneehole bookcase. There is doll's furniture in the bedroom designed for nine-year-old Margaret Tryon, which includes a rare little walnut wing chair.

In Mrs. Tryon's dressing room, one finds a gothic Chippendale mirror, Chelsea-Derby candlesticks, and octagon spectacles owned by Susannah Caswell, daughter of the first state governor.

The supper room contains Chinese Chippendale mahogany furniture. A sofa once owned by the Dowager Duchess of Marlborough is still covered in its original needlework. Also on display is a set of Chinese export tea service.

In the drawing room are Adam inlaid console tables and elbow chairs, Raeburn open-arm chairs, carved and gilded Chippendale mirrors, and a slant-top mahogany desk with bookcase top.

Various antique collections in the Palace are worth noting. Among silver items are a cup and its cover of 1718 by Samuel Pantin, and four candlesticks by Richard Greene dated 1720. Also on view are a coffee pot with side handle of 1721 by Paul de Lamerie, a kettle, stand, and salver dated 1734 by George Hindmarsh, and an epergne (ornamental centerpiece) of 1751 by William Cripps.

Paintings and portraits include original works by Claude Lorrain, Alan Ramsay, Thomas Gainsborough, and Sir Richard Wilson. Royal portraits are from the schools of Sir Godfrey Kneller and Sir Peter Lely.

A collection of small antique objects helps contribute to the lived-in look of the Palace. Among the more interesting artifacts found here are fragments of glass and ceramic wares. Fragments of creamware dominate the ceramic collection, many of them in shapes of the early Wedgwood Queensware moulds. There are examples of practically all of the English wares in then-current use, including redware, salt-glaze pottery, tortoise shellware, delftware, and Chinese porcelain.

The grounds of the Tryon Palace Complex are landscaped in the 18th-century English style. During most of the year, there are daily demonstrations of spinning and weaving on an antique loom and spinning wheel in the Daves House, dating about 1810, which is located on the grounds. Weather permitting, candlemaking and basketmaking are demonstrated outdoors on the grounds.

Van Cortlandt Manor

Van Cortlandt Manor   U.S. Route 9, Croton-on Hudson, NY   (914) 631-8200   Daily: 10-5   Closed New Year's Day, Thanksgiving, and Christmas. Admission: adults $4.00, children $2.50 (combined ticket covering Sunnyside, Philipsburg Manor, and Van Cortlandt Manor $10.00)   Guided tours are 1½ hours.

This early-18th-century, brick-and-stone, Dutch-English manor house with a

piazza and raised porch was the headquarters of the 86,000-acre estate of the powerful Van Cortlandt family of Revolutionary War patriots for 260 years. Although it is now reduced to 20 acres, the manor with its extant ferry house and gardens appears as it did during the Revolutionary War period, recalling 18th-century Hudson River Valley life.

In the early 18th century, the Van Cortlandts lived in New York, using the original part of this house as a hunting lodge and trading post. Not until 1749 was the manor enlarged as a permanent residence for Pierre Van Cortlandt, the third lord of the manor. From that time on, the house became a center of social life and political history. Among notables said to have visited the manor are Benjamin Franklin, John Jay, and George Washington.

The house is filled with original Van Cortlandt family furnishings, porcelain, pewter, silver, and portraits.

On the ground floor, the so-called Old Parlor served as both sitting and dining room. The furniture ranges in date from the late 17th century to the second half of the 18th century and is mainly of Hudson River Valley origin. An 18th-century, New York oval table with a Hudson Valley pad on disc feet is surrounded by four Queen Anne country chairs. Both the curtains and the chair cushions are of 18th-century, blue-and-white, resist-dyed fabric. Hanging on the mantle are rifles and powder horns engraved with maps of the Hudson River, in use during the French and Indian War. A cupboard is filled with English and some Dutch mid-18th-century delftware.

The Kitchen on the ground floor features many Van Cortlandt family possessions. Most notable is the long pine sawbuck table (early trestle table) with X-shaped supports peculiar to New York country tables. It is surrounded by a collection of Queen Anne, Hudson Valley, rush-bottomed chairs (seats made of rushes or reeds, common on turned-wood chairs, and considered to be very durable). An array of pewter plates by the famous London Spackman pewterers is displayed in a Dutch kas (cupboard with a double body, the upper part being open shelves recessed over the bottom doors).

The main, second floor of the manor, which is accessible by a narrow exterior staircase, houses additional family possessions. A black painted armchair made in New York about 1690-1700 is one of the treasured family heirlooms. The half-round mahogany table located in the rear halls bears the label of New York cabinetmaker Elbert Anderson, who was active in the 1790s. A portrait of Joanna Livingston, who married Pierre Van Cortlandt in 1748, was painted by Ezra Ames, an important portraitist of New York families.

The elegant second-floor Parlor contains furniture that ranges from Queen Anne and Chippendale styles to the neoclassical style, that is, from about 1740 to the turn of the 19th century. A New York Chippendale tea table and camelback sofa are on view along with a large selection of Chinese export porcelain from the last half of the 18th century. There are Sheraton side chairs made in New York about 1790. The latest object in the room is the French empire mantel clock from New York.

By the fireplace wall of the Dining Room, the dominant piece of furniture is a massive drop-leaf table of the William and Mary style with a mahogany top dating from about 1800. Its presence documents the first use of mahogany in American furniture. A Chippendale pier looking glass and a Chippendale slab-top mixing table are also displayed along with a New York City mahogany sideboard from 1790-1800. In addition to family pieces of silver, such as a coffeepot made in London in 1763 by William and R. Peaston, there are notable ceramics on view. These include porcelain figurines from the English Chelsea

and Chelsea-Derby factories, as well as Chinese export and Canton porcelain.

The Northeast Bed Chamber contains a Chippendale chest-on-chest (also known as a double chest, whereby the bottom section projected outward from the slightly narrower upper chest mounted upon it). One of the few English pieces of furniture in the manor is the Queen Anne walnut armchair. During the winter, the bed is hung with its original English 18th-century copperplate printed cotton curtains. The cast-iron stove was made in the classical, early Adam style from the mid-18th century.

The Prophet's Chamber, named for the numerous Methodist preachers who slept in it during the late 18th and 19th centuries, exhibits a mahogany dressing table made about 1750-70, which is the only piece of Philadelphia furniture in the family collection. Also on display are an inlaid firescreen and a Chippendale corner chair (an occasional open-back armchair designed to be placed in the corner of a room).

The top floor, reached by a staircase, houses a mahogany Chippendale press cupboard (a cupboard first made in America during the second half of the 17th century and popular in the early 18th century), and a set of chairs in neoclassical style. In addition, there is a neoclassical Pembroke table (an occasional table with a drop-leaf on each side and a drawer set in the apron), which is representative of the simple type of family furniture in the manor house.

The Van Cortlandt Ferry House, a story-and-a-half, brickfronted building, provided shelter for people using the ferry service that carried them across the Croton River without a long detour. It is furnished with such typical Hudson River Valley 18th-century country furniture as hutch tables, Windsor chairs, stoneware, pewter, rush-bottom chairs, and a Dutch kas or cupboard. The Ferry House display offers a view of an 18th-century Hudson Valley Dutch mode of life which is simpler and less sophisticated than that of the more formal Manor.

Vanderbilt Mansion

Vanderbilt Mansion   U.S. Route 9, Hyde Park, NY 12538   (914) 229-9115   Daily: 9-5; grounds remain open until dusk   Closed New Year's Day and Christmas.   Tours are given on the hour and half-hour, 9-4:30; reservations are necessary for groups over ten.   Admission: $1.50 (includes admission to the Franklin D. Roosevelt Home)

About six miles north of Poughkeepsie, the sumptuous Vanderbilt Mansion was once the country home of Frederick W. Vanderbilt, financier and grandson of "Commodore" Cornelius Vanderbilt. It is an outstanding example of the great estates built by wealthy financial and industrial leaders between 1880 and 1900, and is characterized by its Beaux-Arts style of architecture.

Now a National Historic Site, the mansion is the focal point of the estate, which consists of 212 acres on the east bank of the Hudson River, where there are walking trails with scenic views. The mansion was designed by the architectural firm McKim, Mead and White and completed in 1898. Noted decorators Georges A. Glaenzer and Ogden Codman designed the decor of some of the rooms. The mansion's lavish furnishings are predominantly Italian and French Renaissance pieces, dating from the 16th to the 18th centuries.

On the first floor in the Main Hall, where guests were greeted, there are two cabinets from the Italian Renaissance and a tapestry above the fireplace which bears the powerful Florentine Medici family coat of arms. The study, where Frederick Vanderbilt conducted the estate affairs, is paneled in Santo Domingo mahogany. On display are early Italian pistols and an old Flemish clock.

Exterior view of Abigail Adams Smith House.

Latham Memorial Garden at Tryon Palace; one of 18 gardens in complex.

Used as the family living room, the Den is decorated with wood carvings done by Swiss artists. Mrs. Vanderbilt's letterwriting table and Mr. Vanderbilt's favorite chair are displayed. In the South Foyer are 16th-century Brussels tapestries which depict events of the Trojan War.

The Living Room, used for formal entertaining, reveals wall paneling of Circassian walnut from Russia. There are twin fireplaces of Italian marble and French doors. The Reception Room, where guests gathered for sherry before dinner, was designed after an 18th-century French drawing room with its abundant gold-leaf decoration. The ceiling painting was done by American artist Edward E. Simmons in 1897.

In the North Foyer, a 17th-century Brussels tapestry and an 18th-century Aubusson tapestry (a rug with no pile that is woven like a tapestry) may be seen. Two Renaissance mantels are found in the spacious Dining Room, which was the scene of many elaborate parties.

On the second floor in the North Foyer, there are paintings by Schreyer, Villegas, and Bouguereau, who painted Renaissance-type nudes in neoclassical style. Also on display is a Louis XVI (1774-93) table with an Indian incense burner of marble and cloisonne enamel. In the Mauve Room, a guest room, there are mantelpieces of the ornate, neoclassical French Empire period (1804-20) and a Persian dowry rug.

Paintings by Kellar-Reutlinger and Firman-Girard hang in the South Foyer. Louise Vanderbilt's Room is a reproduction of a French queen's bedroom of the rococo Louis XV period (1715-74), and displays hand-embroidered silk on the wall at the head of the bed. In Frederick Vanderbilt's Room, the walls are covered with 17th-century Flemish tapestries. The bed and dresser were designed as part of the woodwork, which is carved Circassian walnut.

White House

The White House   1600 Pennsylvania Ave. NW, Washington D.C 20500 (202) 456-1414   Tuesday-Saturday: 10 a.m.-12 noon   Closed some holidays.   Enter on E. Executive Ave.   Visitors with a physical handicap that will not permit them to use the stairs should go to the North East Gate where wheelchairs are available if needed.

As the office and home of the President of the United States, the White House has been the setting of many great moments in American history. It contains many important American period furnishings and decorative arts from the late 18th and 19th centuries.

The cornerstone of the White House was laid in 1792 on a site selected by President George Washington. Plans for the house were drawn by Irish-born architect James Hoban, who also superintended its construction. The exterior sandstone walls were painted during the course of construction, causing the building to be termed the "White House" from an early date.

The White House was first occupied by President and Mrs. John Adams in 1800, although most of the building's interior had not yet been completed. During Thomas Jefferson's administration, the east and west terraces were constructed. British forces captured Washington and burned the house in 1814, and reconstruction began the following year. The south portico was built in 1824; the large north portico over the entrance and the driveway was completed in 1829.

After Theodore Roosevelt moved into the White House in 1901, its interior was repaired and refurnished the following year by the architectural firm McKim, Mead and White. Several changes were made between 1903 and 1948. Among them, the west wing offices were enlarged in 1909, several guest rooms

Exterior view of the White House (Washington DC).

Readbourne Parlor at Winterthur Museum (Winterthur, DE); one of 196 sitting rooms.

were made in the attic during Woodrow Wilson's presidency, and the roof and third story were remodeled in 1927. In 1948 a balcony was completed off the second floor behind the columns of the south portico.

Between 1948 and 1952, the White House was renovated. The old sandstone walls were retained and supported by concrete foundations, and interior wooden beams and brick supporting walls were replaced by a modern steel framework.

Each room in the White House has its own distinctive style:

The Library   More than 2,700 volumes dealing with important aspects of American life—biography, history, fiction, the sciences, and the humanities—line the floor-to-ceiling shelves. The room contains American furniture of the Federal period, a chandelier once owned by the family of James Fenimore Cooper, and five portraits of American Indians representing a delegation received by President Monroe in 1821.

The Vermeil Room   An entensive display of vermeil (articles of gold over silver) is exhibited on the shelves. Many pieces are used for State luncheons and dinners.

The China Room   This room was first used for the display of china in 1917 by Mrs. Woodrow Wilson. On shelves behind glass are pieces from china settings used by all the past Presidents. The walls of the China Room, as well as those in the Library, are paneled in wood from the 1817 timbers which were replaced with steel girders during the 1948-52 renovation.

The Diplomatic Reception Room   This oval-shaped room is furnished as a parlor of the late 18th or early 19th century. It was from this room that President Franklin Roosevelt made his fireside chats. The wallpaper, printed in France in 1834, depicts several American natural wonders and historic places: Niagara Falls, Boston Harbor, West Point, Natural Bridge of Virginia, and New York Bay.

The State Floor   Furnishings and decorations are predominantly of late 18th- and early 19th-century style. Portraits of many Presidents hang from the walls of the lobby, cross hall, and first-floor rooms.

The East Room   The largest in the White House, this room is used for State receptions, balls, afternoon receptions for varied groups, press conferences, and many other events, including weddings and funerals. The walls are covered by white enameled wood paneling placed in the room by Theodore Roosevelt. There are large cut-glass chandeliers dating from 1902, and an oak parquetry floor. The Steinway concert piano, decorated with folk dancing scenes and eagle supports, was presented in 1938. On the east wall is the most notable portrait in the White House, the Gilbert Stuart painting of George Washington, which Dolly Madison saved when the British burned the house in 1814. A portrait of Martha Washington, painted later, also hangs on the east wall.

The Green Room   Once serving as Thomas Jefferson's dining room, this room has been refurbished as a Federal parlor and is now used for receptions. The American-designed furniture was made in New York by Duncan Phyfe or his contemporaries. On the floor is a 19th-century Turkish Hereke rug, and on a table are a silver coffee urn owned by John Adams and a pair of silver candlesticks used by Dolly Madison. The cut-glass and gilt-bronze chandelier dates from 1810.

The Blue Room   Famous for its beauty and its elliptical shape, the Blue Room is often used by the President to receive guests at State dinners and receptions. The walls are covered with reproduction wallpaper with classical

Mrs. Phipps' bedroom at Old Westbury House.

Montmorenci Stair Hall at Winterthur Museum.

scenes based on a French paper of about 1800. Portraits in this room include *Thomas Jefferson* by Rembrandt Peale, *John Adams* by John Trumbull, and *John Tyler* by G.P.A. Healy.

The Blue Room is furnished to represent the period of James Monroe, who purchased items for the room after the fire of 1814. On the white marble mantel is a Hannibal clock and a pair of French porcelain vases acquired in 1817. Seven of the original Monroe chairs, and four reproduction chairs, are upholstered in blue silk with an American eagle design on the back. The color blue was first used in the room during the administration of Martin Van Buren (1837-41).

The Red Room   Used for small receptions, this room is decorated as an American Empire parlor of 1810-30. The walls and upholsteries are covered with a red twill satin fabric with a gold scroll designed border. On the marble mantel, a duplicate of the Green Room mantel, is a musical clock presented in 1952 by the President of France.

The State Dining Room   The large State Dining Room has floor-to-ceiling English oak paneling, which was originally installed in 1902 by Theodore Roosevelt. A gilded chandelier hangs from the ceiling, and on the wall above the mantel is a portrait of President Abraham Lincoln by G.P.A. Healy.

Lobby and Cross Hall   Six classical marble columns separate the lobby from the cross hall. Over the entrance to the Blue Room is the seal of the President of the United States. Seals of the Thirteen Original States are carved on the marble-faced opening of the stairway. Portraits of recent Presidents may be seen here.

The Second and Third Floors   These floors are reserved for the presidential family and guests. The Lincoln Bedroom, with its massive 8-foot bed purchased during the Civil War, is restored in the Victorian style. Adjoining this room is the Treaty Room, which served as the Cabinet Room from 1865 to 1902. The cabinet table, settee, and clock, purchased by President Grant in 1869, are in this room. The Queen's Bedroom (Rose Guest Room) is furnished as an early 19th-century bedroom.

Grounds   Surrounding the White House are informal, carefully-landscaped grounds. They include flower gardens, lawns, and many trees of historic interest, such as the magnolias planted by President Andrew Jackson and an American elm planted by John Quincy Adams. To the east, the Jacqueline Kennedy Garden displays a sense of the miniature and to the west, the famous Rose Garden is the location of many Presidential ceremonies.

Winterthur Museum

Henry Francis Du Pont Winterthur Museum and Gardens   Route 52, Winterthur, DE 19735   (302) 654-1548   Tuesday-Saturday: 10-4; Sunday, holiday Mondays, and July 4: 12-4   Closed other Mondays and New Year's Day, Thanksgiving, and December 24 and 25.   Admission fees vary; special rates for senior citizens, groups of 25 or more, and students over 16; children under 12 free.   A variety of programs, special events, and reserved and unreserved tours are offered.

Located in Brandywine Valley, six miles northwest of Wilmington, Delaware, Winterthur was the home of Henry Francis du Pont until his death in 1969. In 1951 du Pont moved to a new house nearby and opened his original residence, built in 1839, as a public museum. The museum is widely considered to be the greatest collection of American antiques in the United States.

Beginning as a collector of European antiques, du Pont bought his first piece of Americana—a 1737 Pennsylvania chest—in 1923. Over the decades he accumulated outstanding examples of American woodwork, furniture, textiles,

Exterior-view of Winterthur Museum.

Mahogany Billiard Table, Annapolis (18th century). Winterthur Museum.

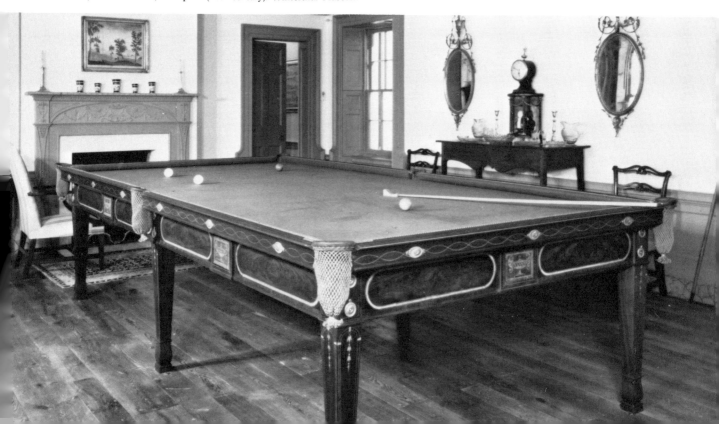

paintings, prints, pewter, silver, ceramics, glass, needlework, and brass. Over 71,000 objects made or used in America between 1640 and 1840 are displayed in 196 room settings in the museum. More than 100 period rooms and other display rooms bring to life almost every level of American society from the simplest to the most elegant.

In addition to the main museum, the George and Martha Washington Wing, added in 1960 and 1971, provide casual visitors with a look at the chronological development of American craftsmanship in the decorative arts of the six style periods included at Winterthur—Seventeenth Century, William and Mary, Queen Anne, Chippendale, Federal, and Empire.

Highlights of the museum include Chippendale furniture by well-known Newport, Rhode Island cabinetmakers John Townsend and John Goddard; six silver tankards by American patriot and master silversmith Paul Revere; and the portrait of George Washington at Verplanck's Point by John Trumbell, who painted personalities and historical pictures of the War of Independence. Also notable are pewter pieces by Philadelphian William Will; a pair of sofas owned by John Dickinson, "penman of the American revolution;" Pennsylvania-German earthenware; and Chinese export porcelain.

Notable among the many display rooms of the museum, the Readbourne Parlor contains Philadelphia chairs of the Queen Anne style as well as a Philadelphia sofa with cabriole legs (furniture legs in the decorative form of an animal's leg). In this room is one of the best examples at Winterthur of colonial America's taste for Chinese ornamentation, the japanned high chest of drawers made by Joshua Pimm of Boston around 1745. In addition, there are silver candlearms by Jacob Hurd of Boston; candlesticks by Nathaniel Morse, who worked in Boston from 1709 to 1748; and wall sconces by John Sanders of London.

The Blackwell Parlor is an excellent example of 18th-century American architecture. Much of the interior structure was imported by du Pont from Philadelphia, where it was part of the original Blackwell House built about 1764. It is furnished in Philadelphia Chippendale dating back to the late 1700s.

The Chinese Parlor features Chinese Chippendale furniture (18th-century rococo furniture influenced by oriental motifs), against a backdrop of wallpaper painted in China about 1770. There is also a Newport sofa made by Adam Coe in 1812, in addition to a Charleston table and a Philadelphia chair.

In the Du Pont Dining Room, French decorative styles can be seen. Hanging at the window are blue lampas (similar to damask fabric, generally embroidered) curtains woven in France from designs by Phillippe de Lassalle, court textile designer to Louis XVI. Also on view is a mahogany dining table from Boston, which is accompanied by mahogany chairs from a set made in New York for Victor Marie du Pont.

The Phyfe Room is devoted to works of New York cabinetmaker Duncan Phyfe, known for early works in the classic Adam tradition, and later for work that reflects the American Regency style. On view are ten side chairs, two armchairs, a caned settee, a sofa table, and tripod-based card tables among other items.

Like the museum, the 200-acre public gardens of Winterthur are a legacy of Henry Francis du Pont, who was primarily responsible for the present appearance of the estate. The gardens represent a historic period landscape and contain horticulturally significant collections of plants, which can be appreciated best with the changing seasons. There are thousands of varieties of plants, from native wildflowers to exotic trees and shrubs from all over the

world, all landscaped in the English style.

Adjacent to the museum, the Louise du Pont Crowninshield Research Building contains a library, scientific laboratories, and conservation facilities. The library, which is open to the public, houses one of the most complete collections of printed, manuscript, photographic, microfilm, and archival research materials for the study of the decorative arts and material culture in the United States prior to 1914. The public is invited to bring objects to monthly clinics on conservation and object identification. Reproductions of museum objects and Winterthur publications as well as various books relating to the museum's collections are available for sale.

Blackwell Parlor at Winterthur Museum. Furnished in Philadelphia Chippendale (late 18th century).

Book II
The Galleries

Art
Galleries

Art Galleries

By Location

California
Beverly Hills:
   Petersen
Carmel:
   Galerie De Tours
Encino:
   Redfern
Los Angeles:
   Goldfield, Pink
San Francisco:
   Iannetti, North Point
Illinois
Chicago:
   Branca, Campanile, Johnson,
Mongerson, Sternberg
Maryland
Bethesda:
   Montrose
Massachusetts
Boston:
   Childs, Lowe
New York
New York City:
A.C.A., Childs, Colnaghi, Findlay,
Goldschmidt, Grossman, Hirschl &
Adler, Jeffrey Alan, Kennedy, Lux, Old
Print Shop, Pannonia, Schweitzer,
Smith, Spanierman, St. Etienne, Terry-
Engell, York
Pennsylvania
Philadelphia:
   David, Newman, Schwarz
Texas
Fort Worth:
   Hall
Houston:
   James-Atkinson
Virginia
Alexandria:
   Liros
Washington DC
   Hom, Hull, Old Print Gallery, Taggert &
Jorgensen

By Specializations

American Paintings:
   A.C.A., Campanile, Childs, David,
   Galerie De Tours, Findlay, Goldfield,
   Hall, Hirschl & Adler, Hom, Hall,
   James-Atkinson, Jeffrey Alan, Kennedy
   Liros, Lux, Mongerson, Montrose,
   Newman, North Point, Petersen,
   Redfern, Schweitzer, Smith,
   Spanierman, Surovek, St. Etienne,
   Sternberg, Taggert & Jorgensen, Valley
   House, York
French Paintings:
   Findlay, Goldschmidt, Grossman, Hall,
   Hirschel & Adler, James-Atkinson,
   Schweitzer, Terry-Engell
Italian Paintings:
   Colnaghi
Marine Paintings:
   Lowe, Smith
European Paintings:
   Childs, David, Galerie De Tours,
   Goldschmidt, Grossman, Hom, Pasquale
   Iannetti, James-Atkinson, Liros, Lux,
   Newman, Pannonia, Redfern,
   Schweitzer, Schwarz, St. Etienne,
   Sternberg, Taggert & Jorgensen, Valley
   House
Prints:
   Branca, Childs, Goldschmidt, Johnson,
   Old Print Gallery, Old Print Shop, Pink,
   Redfern

A.C.A. Galleries   21 E. 67th St., New York, NY 10021   (212) 628-2440   ***A.C.A.***
Tuesday-Saturday: 10-5:30; July-August: Tuesday-Friday: 10-5

Established over 50 years ago, A.C.A. Galleries features three centuries of American painting. The 18th- and 19th-century selections emphasize American impressionists John Twachtman, Childe Hassam and Ernest Lawson, as well as late Hudson River school and luminist painter Martin Johnson Heade and landscapist John F. Kensett. Additional outstanding artists of this period on exhibit are William Merritt Chase, Frederick Church, John Singleton Copley, Thomas Eakins, Willard Leroy Metcalf, Mary Cassatt, and Frederick Waugh.

Other American masters featured include members of the Ash Can school of realist painters, notably Robert Henri, George Luks, Everett Shinn and William Glackens. American masters belonging to the Stieglitz group, namely Max Weber and Georgia O'Keeffe are also displayed.

Branca Prints   67 East Oak, Chicago, IL 60611   (312) 751-2017   ***Branca***
Tuesday-Friday: 10:30-6, Saturday: 11-4

This Oak Street gallery features decorative European prints dating from the 16th through the 19th centuries. The collection includes hand-colored botanical, natural history, architectural, and costume prints as well as portraits and landscapes. The gallery showcases works by known and unknown European artists. Among the artists represented are Pierre-Joseph Redoute (flowers), John Gould (birds), Mark Catesby (natural history and botanicals), William Curtis (botanicals), and H.L. Duhamel du Monceau (botanicals and fruit). Also included are George Edwards (birds), Pancrace Bessa (fruits), Compte de Buffon (natural history), N. Mortier (architecturals), and Colen Campbell (architecturals). Denis Diderot is represented by all subjects, notably military, nautical, and natural history themes.

The gallery's antique prints were originally engraved illustrations for rare books and portfolios. It was not until the 19th century that people actually began collecting prints for display. Through the years, antique prints have made a significant contribution to the study of nature, architecture, and customs.

Campanile   Campanile Galleries   200 S. Michigan Ave., Chicago, IL 60604   (312) 622-7010   Monday-Friday: 9-5:30; Saturday: 9:30-4

Located across from the Art Institute of Chicago, the gallery offers American paintings from the late 18th to the early 20th centuries as well as drawings and small-scale sculptures. Many of the works are acquired from the estates of artists.

The gallery houses four major exhibitions per year, usually centering around 19th-century American masters, many of whom worked in the impressionist vein. Among those shown are members of "The Ten," a group of American painters, mostly Easterners, who studied in France and brought the *plein air* style back to this country. Guy Wiggins' landscapes and harbor scenes show an affinity to some of Monet's works as do the canvases of Theodore Butler, who married the haystack painter's stepdaughter and absorbed his father-in-law's loosely brushed style and soft atmosphere. Childe Hassam, who passed through an impressionist and a post impressionist phase, is shown in both of his periods. The gallery also shows paintings of the Ash Can school of realism's "Immortal Eight," including Arthur B. Davies, William Glackens, Ernest Lawson, Maurice Prendergast, John Sloan, Robert Henri, George Lukas, and Everett Shinn.

The gallery has diversified its collection to include some fine decorative pieces such as an Empire Regency desk in mahogany and a matching cabinet, an 18th-century oak library table, and an Italian baroque gilt table with a marble top. Also included are antique and semi-antique jewelry, with rings, earrings, bracelets, and necklaces. Glassware in cobalt blue, cranberry glass and cut crystal are also exhibited. In addition, bronze sculptures by contemporary artist Clemente Spanipinato are shown exclusively here.

Childs   Childs Gallery   169 Newbury St., Boston, MA 02116, and 956 Madison Ave., New York, NY 10021   (617) 266-1108 and (212) 772-6606   Tuesday-Saturday: 10-5

The gallery was founded in 1937 by Charles D. Childs, who has been dealing in fine American and European 18th-, 19th- and early 20th-century paintings, prints, and drawings. Childs recently opened a branch in New York City where the full range of his inventory can be seen as well.

American paintings continue to be the gallery's specialty. Childs is known in 18th century American painting and for rediscoveries in American art. Well-represented artists are John Singleton Copley, John Smibert, Joseph Badger, Charles Wilson Peale, and John Trumbull in the 18th century; Robert Salmon, Fitz Hugh Lane, William Sidney Mount, George Caleb Bingham, Albert Bierstadt, and Winslow Homer in the 19th century; and, "The Eight" (the Ash Can school of realist painters, namely Robert Henri, William Glackens, George Luks, John Sloan, Everett Shinn, Maurice Prendergast, Arthur Davies, and Ernest Lawson), "The Ten" (a group of American impressionist painters, including John Twachtman, Childe Hassam, and J. Alden Weir), members of the Boston school and other artists of the American scene in the 20th century. In addition, Childs seeks out fine works by less well-known artists.

The print department at Childs has always been an important interest. In addition to old master specialties of Rembrandt and Durer, prints of the etching revival of 1850-1950 in America, Britain, and Europe are strong. The sporting etchings of Frank Benson, A.L. Ripley, and Roland Clark form an important concentration within the department.

E.H. Blashfield, *A Modern Rebbecca,* 36″ x 24″, oil on canvas. James-Atkinson Gallery (Houston).

The newer drawing and watercolor department is nearly comprehensive in its holdings of American drawings. Copley, John Singer Sargent, George Bellows, George Luks, William Sidney Mount, and Eastman Johnson are a few of the names that are represented. Major works in watercolor by Homer, Prendergast and Charles Burchfield, are regularly available.

Colnaghi

Colnaghi   26 E. 80th St., New York, NY 10021   (212) 722-2266
Monday-Saturday: 10-6

This firm traces its history back to 1760 when an Italian pyrotechnist, Giovanni Battista Torre, opened a shop in Paris called Cabinet de Physique. Paul Colnaghi, who later acquired the shop, was appointed the Prince Regent's print seller and employed to arrange the royal collection, adding drawings and watercolors of the English school. By the 1930s the firm changed hands and published etchings and drypoints along with trading old master paintings. In 1982 a new American branch of the gallery opened in New York. Among the works shown in the collection were Giovanni Bellini's *St. Francis in Ecstasy,* Titian's *Pietro Aretino* (now in the Frick Collection) Botticelli's *Virgin and Child* (now in the Isabella Stewart Gardner Museum) and others. Also handled were paintings by such artists as Jan Van Eyck, Raphael, Peter Paul Reubens and Rembrandt which are now in major international museums.

In recent years Colnaghi has held exhibitions in the field of 17th and 18th-century painting. The most important include "Sebastiano Ricci" in 1978 and "Florentine Painting 1600-1700," presented at the Royal Academy in 1979. Over the past five years, the gallery has also handled sculpture, furniture, and works of art, a departure from its usual inventory.

David David

David David, Inc.   260 S. 18th St., Philadelphia, PA 19103   (215) 735-2922   Monday-Friday: 10-5

Established in 1910 by David David, the gallery is carried on in the family tradition by the founder's grandsons. Located in a townhouse of 1880 adjacent to Rittenhouse Square, the gallery deals in paintings, drawings, and sculpture from the 16th through the early 20th centuries. Although both European and American schools are represented, the Davids concentrate on American paintings. The large inventory of American impressionist paintings includes works by William Merritt Chase, Carl Frieseke, Maurice Prendergast, Martha Walker, Mary Cassatt, and John Twachtman. Hudson River school artists exhibited are Albert Bierstadt, Frederick Church, Thomas Cole, and Jasper Cropsey. There are also mid-18th-century Colonial painters such as Charles Willson Peal, John Singleton Copley, Gilbert Stuart, and Thomas Sulley. Also displayed are works by still-life artists Serern Roesen, John Pieto, James Raphael Peale, and William Harnett as well as landscape paintings by Barbizon school artists George Inness, William Keith, and Homer Martin. Master painters of the American West, such as Frederic Remington, Thomas Moran, and Charles Russell, are also on hand.

European artists represented at the gallery include Camille Corot and Charles Daubigny, Auguste Renoir, Max Luce, Claude Monet and Camille Pissarro along with the Victorian masters James Tissot, Sir Edward Burne-Jones, Henry Pether and William Mc Taggart. There are also examples of 17th-century genre paintings by Salomon van Ruysdale, Jan van Goyen, and Franz Post.

William M. Chase, *Portrait of Miss F. DeForest,* 20″ x 16″, oil on canvas. Richard York Gallery (New York).

Sculpture at the gallery is mostly 18th and 19th-century French pieces, including some small works by Auguste Rodin and Edgar Degas. There is a Kuiba bust of Shakespeare and some examples from the Neo-Classical period.

De Tours Galerie De Tours   P.O. Box 4996, Carmel CA 93921   (408) 624-3763   Daily: 10:30-5

The firm has four galleries on the West Coast specializing in 19th-century American paintings with a good representation of European paintings. Historical paintings of the American West are emphasized.

Key American works shown are by artists Albert Bierstadt and Asher B. Durand of the Hudson River school of landscape painting, Robert Henri of the Ash Can school of realism, impressionist F. Childe Hassam, genre painter Eastman Johnson, independent narrative artist Winslow Homer, and Frederic Remington, who recorded the life of the cowboys, the plains Indians, and the open range of the American West.

Included in the European collection are examples of Henry Harpignies, Henri Lebasque, Charles Camoin, Maurice Utrillo, Pierre Bonnard, Eugene Boudin, Armand Guillaumin, S. Lepine, Edouard Vuillard, and others.

The gallery also handles bronze and marble sculpture by Auguste Rodin, Pierre Auguste Renoir, and Frederic Remington in addition to many other sculptors. Special exhibitions are held six times per year.

David Findlay David Findlay Galleries   984 Madison Ave. at 77th St., New York, NY 10021   (212) 249-2909   Monday-Saturday: 10-5

The gallery was founded in Kansas City in 1870 and moved to New York in 1937. It exhibits 19th and early 20th-century French and American paintings, contemporary French paintings, and contemporary American paintings and graphics.

Artists included in the gallery's collection of 19th and 20th-century paintings are Childe Hassam, Fantin-Latour, Irving Couse, Henry Farny, Armand Guillaumin, Eugene Boudin, Martin Johnson Heade, George Inness, Johan Berthold, Gustave Loiseau, Willard Metcalf, Thomas Moran, Severin Roesen, Andre Segonzac, and Charles M. Russell.

Among contemporary French artists represented are Bernard Cathelin, Pierre Lesieur, Maurice Brianchon, Roger Muhl, Rene Genis and Bardone, who are all post-Impressionist painters from the Paris school. A catalogue of 19th-century works is available.

Goldfield Goldfield Galleries   8400 Melrose Ave., Los Angeles, CA 90069   (213) 651-1122   Monday-Saturday: 11-4

Goldfield Galleries specializes in Western artists, American Impressionists, and other important American artists of the 19th and 20th centuries.

The gallery features the primary American impressionists: Frank W. Benson, Joseph R. DeCamp, Thomas W. Dewing, F. Childe Hassam, Willard L. Metcalf, Robert L. Reid, Edward E. Simmons, Edmund C. Tarbell, John H. Twachtman, J. Alden Weir, and William Merritt Chase. The famous realistic painters of the Ash Can school who are shown include Arthur B. Davies, William Glackens, Robert Henri, Ernest Lawson, George Luks, Maurice Prendergast, Everett Shinn, John Sloan, Jerome Myers, and Robert Spencer. The Western scene is depicted by Frederic Remington, Charles M. Russell, William R. Leigh, William Gollings, E. I. Couse, J. H. Sharp, E. Martin

John Singer Sargent, *Mrs. Louis E. Raphael,* 57″ x 38″, oil on canvas. Kennedy Galleries (New York).

Hennings, O. E. Berninghaus, and Victor Higgins.

Other artists include Albert Bierstadt, 19th-century landscape artist; Thomas Hart Benton, American regionalist famous for Midwestern farm and country scenes; and Stanton MacDonald Wright and Morgan Russell, two of the foremost early modern artists. Also represented are Edgar Payne, a California painter currently enjoying vast popularity; Charles Hawthorne, turn-of-the-century figure painter of unique style; Guy Pene du Bois, an artist and critic who provided social commentary of the twenties; and Reginald Marsh, famous for his realistic paintings of the seamy side of the Bowery and the Lower East Side of New York.

Lucien Goldschmidt

Lucien Goldschmidt Inc.   1117 Madison Ave., New York, NY 10028   (212) 879-0070   Monday-Friday: 10-6, Saturday: 10-5

The gallery represents graphic art from Albrecht Durer to Picasso, Henri Matisse, and Jacques Villon. It emphasizes not only famous artists like Rembrandt, Goya, and Henri de Toulouse-Lautrec, but also many printmakers of French, Italian, German, and Dutch schools. Illustrated catalogues are issued at regular intervals.

Exhibitions of both original drawings and prints from 1500 to 1950 are held. Most recently on view were designs by the Navone brothers executed for a Roman theatre in 1791, and *Pasiphae,* ninety linoleum cuts by Matisse, which were not printed until 1981 and were first displayed at the gallery.

The owner has a special interest in works by Piranesi, French and Italian mannerists and Jacques Villon, as well as in ornament prints and architectural drawings. The gallery also specializes in old and modern illustrated books as well as French literature in first editions.

Daniel B. Grossman

Daniel B. Grossman, Inc./Fine Art   1100 Madison Ave., New York, NY 10028   (212) 861-9285   Monday-Saturday: 10-6

The entire collection of this small, intimate gallery consists of works by artists active in the period 1820 to 1920. Typical works by leading artists of the various schools of the period are displayed in the gallery's two viewing rooms. French landscape paintings of the Barbizon school by its leaders, Charles F. Daubigny and Narcisse V. Diaz de la Pena form a strong part of the collection. The parallel plein-air tradition is also represented by works of E. Sanchez-Perrier in France and J. Maris in Holland. German landscapes that have been exhibited include paintings by J. C. C. Dahl and L. H. T. Gurlitt.

The gallery has strong examples of American still-life paintings by such artists as William M. Harnett and impressionist A. F. Graves. Genre scenes in realistic styles including those by German Liebl, Frenchman F. Bonvin, and Italian C. A. Detti complement the academic Salon of Paris figurative works by A. W. Bouguereau, A. Cabanel, and G. Seignac. Impressionist and post-impressionist paintings show a variety of styles from the Belle Epoque portraits by G. Clairin and E. Toudouze, to the mystical Symbolist works of J. J. Henner, the expressionistic landscapes of M. Denis, and portraits by L. Corinth. Occasional examples of English landscapes, German Nazarene paintings and Oriental scenes are also displayed.

Hall

Hall Galleries   312 Main St., Fort Worth, TX 76102   (817) 322-3773 Monday-Saturday: 10-5:30

Ron Hall, an established Fort Worth dealer in museum-quality 19th- and

Emilio Sanchez-Perrier, *Pontoise,* oil on panel. Daniel B. Grossman Fine Art (New York).

Abbot Fuller Graves, *Still Life with White Roses,* 40″ x 50″, oil on canvas,
Daniel B. Grossman Fine Arts (New York).

20th-century art, has recently moved his gallery to the renovated Conn building in Sundance Square in downtown Fort Worth. The architecture of the turn-of-the-century brownstone-type structure provides a dramatic setting for Hall's changing inventory of paintings by American and French master artists. Hall personally collects and selects works from the Hudson River school, the luminist movement, the Western landscape genre, the American impressionists, and the French post-Impressionists. He has sold major works by Charles Russell, Thomas Moran, Mary Cassatt, George Inness, Robert Reid, Frank Benson, Georgia O'Keeffe, Peter Hurd, and Albert Bierstadt.

Although most of Hall's selections are oils on canvas or board, his inventory includes watercolors, pastels, and occasionally artists' lithographs.

Recent special exhibits included one on Texas folk art and one on contemporary Santa Fe artists.

Hirschl

Hirschl & Adler Galleries   21 E. 70th St., New York, NY 10021   (212) 535-8810   Tuesday-Friday: 9:30-5:30; Saturday: 9:30-5   June, July & September: Monday-Friday: 9:30-5   August: by appointment only

The gallery maintains an encyclopedic collection of 18th and 19th century European paintings as well as American works ranging from the mid-eighteenth century through the 1950s.

The collection of American art includes portraits by John Singleton Copley, still-life paintings by William Harnett and figuratives scenes by Eastman Johnson. Also featured are detailed landscapes by painters of the Hudson River school, such as Albert Bierstadt and Jasper Cropsey. Luminist landscapes by Martin Johnson Heade and Fitz Hugh Lane may also be seen as well as cityscapes by realist painters of "The Eight," including Robert Henri, John Sloan, George Luks, Everett Shinn, and William Glackens. Watercolors by Winslow Homer are also available.

Works by French Impressionists and Post-Impressionists, namely Camille Pissarro, Pierre Bonnard and Paul Gauguin, contribute to the magnitude of the gallery's holdings.

The gallery moved to this landmark building which houses their expanding collection. The building, designed by William Rogers, was a residence when erected in 1918. In 1970 it was renovated to house a modern art gallery and now includes sophisticated lighting and atmospheric controls. The elegant interior creates a quiet, subtle mood which focuses the viewer's attention on the paintings.

Hom

Hom Gallery   2103 O St. NW, Washington, D.C. 20037   (202) 466-4976 Tuesday-Saturday: 11-5

This world-class print gallery specializes in turn-of-the-century European masters like Matisse, Gauguin, Cezanne, Toulouse-Lautrec, Paul Klee and Edvard Munch, as well as early 20th-century American masters like John Sloan, Martin Lewis, Max Weber, Maurice Prendergast, James McNeill Whistler, Childe Hassam, Edward Hopper, Elie Nadelman, and Louis Lozowick. The gallery sometimes carries drawings, paintings, and sculpture by these artists as well.

Leonard Cave, the gallery's only contemporary artist, works in wood and marble sculpture. Other contemporary artists may be added in this new space, which quadruples the gallery's former P St. quarters. Though the gallery will continue to focus on the graphic arts, Hom also plans to expand into more works on paper and paintings.

A highly respected dealer in the Washington area for sixteen years, Hom publishes an annual catalog of his inventory. He often represents the interests of museums, other dealers, and collectors at print auctions all over the world.

William A. Bouguereau, *Venus and Cupid* (1877), 45″ x 20″, oil on canvas.
Pannonia Gallery/Lisa Schiller Fine Art. (New York).

Hull   Hull Gallery   3301 New Mexico Ave., NW, Washington, DC 20016   (202) 362-0507   Monday-Saturday: 10-5:30

Established in 1977, the gallery exhibits 19th- and early 20th-century American art with a concentration on small pieces, mainly watercolors, drawings, and prints. The gallery also maintains a sizeable inventory of works by major artists of this period, which are sometimes displayed.

The early 20th-century American works feature artists such as Childe Hassam, Everett Shinn, William Glackens, George Bellows, Charles Burchfield, Oscar Bluemner, Reginald Marsh, Charles Demuth, Arthur Dove, and Max Weber. Hudson River School painter Alfred T. Bricher is presented as well as the landscape painter Sanford R. Gifford and the seascape artist William T. Richards.

Pasquale Iannetti   Pasquale Iannetti Inc., Art Gallery   575 Sutler St., San Francisco, CA 94102   (415) 433-2771   Monday-Saturday: 10-6

The gallery is owned and directed by Pasquale Iannetti, a Florentine art dealer. He has assembled an unusual collection of fine original prints, drawings, and paintings from the 16th century to the present.

The major focus of the gallery is original prints: etchings, engravings, woodcuts, and lithographs. Works regularly displayed include prints by Rembrandt such as "Descent from the Cross," "The Hundred Guilder Print," and the "Self-portrait with Velvet Cap and Plume." Other old master artists shown are Jacques Callot, the 17th-century French master of spectacles, fairs, and scenes of his time; Lucas van Leyden, known for his superb draughtsmanship and inventiveness in topics common to 16th-century northern Europe; Honore Daumier, the 18th-century French political satirist; and Francisco Goya; Spain's most profound commentator on the human condition of the late 18th and early 19th centuries.

Works of the turn of the 20th century and the Belle Epoque are also displayed. Works by James Tissot, Edgar Chahine, and Paul Cesar Helleu and posters by Jules Cheret and Eugene Samuel Grasset fill the gallery with a sense of the time and an abundance of color.

Additional works are Picasso's etchings, linocuts, and ceramics, Toulouse-Lautrec's lithographs and lithographic posters, Paul Gauguin's woodcuts, Kathe Kollwitz's graphics, as well as works by Paul Signac, Joan Miro, Henri Matisse and Rene Magritte.

James-Atkinson   James-Atkinson Ltd   2015 E. West Gray, Houston, TX 77019   (713) 527-8061   Tuesday-Friday: 10:30-3:30; Saturday 11-4

The gallery has been located near downtown Houston in the River Oaks Center since 1976. It was first established in 1969 in Lake Forest, Illinois, a suburb of Chicago, by Paul Atkinson and his late wife Nancy James. Many of the works presented were acquired at prestigious galleries and auction houses in London and New York.

The gallery carries paintings dating from 1800 to 1900 including French impressionists and British Victorian pieces. American and European works from the 19th century are also presented on both the upper and lower levels. In addition, the upstairs gallery exhibits prints and antique engravings dating from the 18th century to the 19th century.

Various well known artists have been represented here. Among the French impressionists are Charles Agard, Henri Martin, Achilles Lauge, and Paul

Oliver Clare, *Plums, 10″ x 12″*, oil on canvas. James Atkinson Gallery (Houston).

Signac. The American impressionists include Thomas Wilmer Dewing, Ernest Lawson, Theodore Robinson, Mary Cassatt, and John Singer Sargent. Among the many noteworthy British artists on exhibit are John Duncan Fergusson and Ethel Walker. The gallery has also exhibited the work of Dutch painter Eugene Verboeckhoven.

The James-Atkinson gallery holds five traditional exhibitions each year, most of which consist of antique British paintings. In the past the gallery has shown many works by early 19th-century English impressionists from the Cooling Gallery, London, which was established in 1797.

Jeffrey Alan

Jeffrey Alan Gallery   1568 Second Ave., New York, NY 10028   (212) 744-4070   Tuesday-Saturday: 11-6

This informal gallery, located just blocks from the Metropolitan Museum of Art, welcomes browsers and even serves tea. The gallery's inventory features 19th- and early 20th-century American paintings from 1830 to 1930. Landscapes, portraits, and marine and genre paintings are represented by a variety of artists such as George Inness, George Harvey, John Francis Murphy, Hobart Nichols, Jasper Cropsey, E. W. Perry, Bruce Crane, and A. B. Frost. Inness, G. H. Smillie, and G. Harvey are included in the collection of Hudson River School painters. American impressionists include J. Greenwood, W. G. Gaul and J. J. Enneking. Painters from the tonalist school are represented by J. F. Murphy, B. Crane, Leonard Ochtman and F. R. Green. Still lifes from the period include works by George Henry Hall, John Arnold, Benjamin Champney, and Adelaide Palmer. Examples of marine paintings by Alfred Bricher and Antonio Jacobsen and genre works by Frank Duveneck, Enoch Wood Perry, Henry Bacon, and William Morris Hunt are also among the works on view.

In addition to paintings, one can see watercolors by such artists as A. T. Bricher, F. Luis Mora and T. Anshutz. Selections of drawings by Reginald Marsh, George Luks, Francesca Alexander and William Paxton are to be found as well as a few small bronzes by H. K. Brown.

R. S. Johnson

R. S. Johnson International   645 N. Michigan Ave., Chicago, IL 60611 (312) 943-1661   Monday-Saturday: 9-5:30

A spacious place accessible through the Erie Street entrance of the modern Blair Building, this second-floor gallery features great works from historical and contemporary periods. Director R. Stanley Johnson is one of the world's major dealers of old master prints and drawings (1450-1800), and 19th-century prints and drawings (1800-1900). Most of his large and impressive collection can be viewed in the gallery at most times.

Not all the works are on exhibit, but Johnson presents comprehensive shows and has many works in stock. He personally researches and writes the elaborate exhibition catalogs. Past shows included 70 lithographs by Henri de Toulouse-Lautrec, 110 etchings by the Italian architect Pirenesi, and 60 etchings by the Spanish artist Francisco de Goya.

Acquisitions include important works by the French expressionists and impressionists, including Honore Daumier, Maurice Vlaminck, Jacques Villon, Georges Rouault, Odilon Redon, and Vallotton. There are masterpieces by German expressionists such as Emil Nolde, Ernst Kirchner, and Max Beckmann.

Other important gallery exhibitions have included the paintings and

Arthur Burdett Frost, *Holding the fort on Slatlers Hill*, 9″ x 15″, pen and ink.
Jeffrey Alan Gallery (New York).

Charles E. Burchfield, *Fading November Sun*, 30″ x 43″, watercolor. Kennedy Galleries (New York).

drawings of Fernand Leger, the surrealistic paintings of Giorgio De 'Chiricio, works by Picasso (four shows), and works by American artist Mary Cassatt.

The objects of interest to Johnson are beautiful, rare, and by artists of great art historical importance. Works of art are also furnished to a great number of major American museums.

Kennedy

Kennedy Galleries   40 W. 57th St., New York, NY 10019   (212) 541-9600
Tuesday-Saturday: 9:30-5:30; Summer: Monday-Friday: 9:30-5:30

The gallery deals in 18th-, 19th-, and 20th-century American paintings, watercolors, sculpture, and drawings. An inventory of over 25,000 works emphasizes the nineteenth century. Notables in this group include Albert Bierstadt, George Caleb Bingham, David Blythe, William Merritt Chase, Thomas Cole, and John Stuart Curry. Also included are Thomas Dewing, Thomas Doughty, Thomas Eakins, Francis Edmonds, William Harnett, Martin Johnson Heade, and Winslow Homer. Other important artists of the 19th century represented in the gallery's collection are George Inness, Eastman Johnson, John Kensett, Theodore Robinson, John LaFarge, Frederick E. Church, Robert Salmon and Elihu Vedder. The 18th century is represented by portraitists John Singleton Copley, C. W. Peale, John Neagle, Gilbert Stuart, John Trumbull, and John Wollaston.

Liros

Liros Gallery   626 N. Washington St., Alexandria, VA 22314   (703) 549-7881   Monday-Saturday: 10-5:30

Established in 1966, this gallery specializes in 18th- and 19th-century English and American paintings and watercolors. Among the 19th-century American artists represented are landscape artists H. B. Brown, James Hamilton, and G. W. Nicholson. Also displayed are English 18th- and 19th-century works by William Langley, Robert Franklin and landscape painter Jane Nasmith.

The gallery handles 19th-century lithographs by Currier and Ives as well as hand-colored lithographs by F. F. Palmer. Greenbrier icons are available as are Russian and Greek 18th-century icons. Also shown at Liros are old prints such as engravings and chromolithographs of landscapes, vignettes, botanicals, and seascapes. Hand-colored maps dating from 1740 are also displayed.

Albert Bierstadt, *Wasatch Mountains*, 30″ x 40″, oil on canvas.
Richard York Gallery (New York).

Edward Hopper, *Vermont Sugar House,* 13″ x 19″, watercolor. Kennedy Galleries (New York).

Winslow Homer, *Sea and Rocks during a Storm* (1894), 16″ x 22″, watercolor. Kennedy Galleries (New York).

Samuel L. Lowe

Samuel L. Lowe, Jr. Antiques Inc.   80 Charles St., Boston MA 02114   (617)
742-0845   Monday-Friday: 10:30-5, Saturday: 10:30-4   Summer:
Monday-Friday: 10:30-5

This gallery was founded in 1964 by a long-time marine collector. Evidence of
his love is found througout the gallery. Paintings concentrate on whaling,
yachting, ships, and naval scenes as does the collection of prints the gallery
handles. Also to be found are models of whale ships, as well as models of other
ships. There are nautical instruments on hand such as telescopes, compasses,
clocks, bells, ship lanterns, quadrants, sextants, and log slates. Some folk art is
also displayed including carvings, weathervanes, and shop signs. Lead soldiers
and Eskimo scrimshaw (engraved and carved whalebone, whale teeth and
walrus tusk, popular with sailors as an activity) are exhibited here.

Out-of-print books on many of these subjects are a specialty of the gallery.
Out-of-print books on whaling, yachting, and the construction and design of
ship models, as well as naval books and manuscript logs are all among the
collection. The gallery also has a collection of Chinese export porcelain. Plates,
dishes, cups, and saucers from ships or with ship designs predominate. There are
Chinese paintings and prints as well. Because the gallery deals basically in
Americana, the majority of the items here are purchased locally.

Kenneth Lux

Kenneth Lux Gallery   1021 Madison Ave., New York, NY 10021   (212)
861-6839   Tuesday-Saturday: 10-5, Monday: by appointment

For the past 20 years, this gallery has been dealing in 19th and early
20th-century paintings concentrating primarily on American works. Many
different schools of 19th and early 20th-century American art are represented.
Works from the Hudson River school include such artists as Jasper Cropsey,
Frederick Church, David Johnson, Thomas Cole and Asher B. Durand. The
tonalists are represented by Dwight Tryon and Bruce Craine, and
impressionists by Childe Hassam, John Twachtman, Ernest Lawson and
Maurice Prendergast, a member of the Ash Can School. One can also see genre
and story-telling paintings as well.

Another important part of the gallery is the collection of 19th-century
European paintings. Figure painters Jerome Bougauou and Meissonier of the
Paris Salon are shown here. Barbizon painters Narcisse Diaz de la Pena,
Camille Corot, and Theodore Rousseau are usually displayed. The only formal
exhibition the gallery holds is in October and it is always accompanied by a
catalogue.

Mongerson

Mongerson Gallery   620 N. Michigan Ave., Chicago, IL 60611   (312)
943-2354   Monday-Friday: 10-5

The specialty of the gallery is art of the American West, although a good
selection of American impressionist and realistic art is also offered. The
collection of Western American art includes paintings as well as sculptures of
Indians, cowboys, and other folk symbols.

Unlike many galleries, there are no changing monthly exhibitions. When
Mel and Susan Mongerson collect enough of a particular artist's work, they
hold an exhibition. Artists whose work has been displayed in the gallery are N.
C. and Andrew Wyeth, Frank C. McCarthy, and the works of Richard Haley
Lever. There are fine paintings by American impressionist Frederic
Remington. One of Mongerson's main areas of concentration is Western Art by
deceased artists. This includes paintings by members of the Taos ten,

Henry Farney, *A Moment of Suspence,* 12″ x 8″ gouache. Ira Spanierman Gallery (New York).

including Walter Ufer, E. C. Couse, O. E. Berninghaus, Victor Higgins and Martin Hennings.

Montrose

Montrose Galleries   Suite 205, 7800 Wisconsin Ave., Bethesda, MD   (301) 652-4199   Wednesday-Saturday: 12:30-5:30 and by appointment   August: closed

American paintings of the 19th and 20th centuries are the specialty here, with a sub-specialty in Washington painters who worked in this city early on but have only recently been rediscovered. Max Weyl, a turn-of-the-century German immigrant-watchmaker who painted scenes of Rock Creek Park, is but one of many.

Artists whose works have frequently appeared in the gallery include Albert Bierstadt, George Inness, marine painter Frederick J. Waugh, Edwin Lord Weeks, George Hollingsworth, Harry Ives Thompson, and Chester Loomis.

The gallery has a conservator on staff who also offers private restoration services. Long-time collector Henry Glassie is the proprietor.

Newman

Newman Galleries   1625 Walnut St., Philadelphia, PA 19103   (215) 563-1779   Monday-Friday: 9-5:30; Saturday; 10-4:30   July & August: Monday-Friday: 9-5

In its 117th year of participation in the art community, Newman Galleries has locations in Philadelphia and on the Main Line in suburban Bryn Mawr. A wide selection in all media is offered. The collection comprises paintings from the 19th century to contemporary prints. Among the 19th- and 20th-century oil painters from both America and Europe are Thomas Buttersworth, Albert Bierstadt, Thomas Hill, Severin Roesen, Anthony Thieme, and William Trost Richards. Works by renowned portrait painters of the 19th and early 20th centuries are also available. Early 20th-century American artists such as Daniel Garber, Edward Redfield, Fern Coppedge, Fred Wagner, and Frederick Judd Waugh are always a major focus of the collection.

Also exhibited are the works of several American illustrators, namely N. C. Wyeth, F. Sands Brunner, Maurice Bower, and Robert Crowther. The gallery maintains a conservation department for cleaning and repairing works of art.

North Point

North Point Gallery   872 North Point St., San Francisco, CA 94109   (415) 771-3548   Tuesday-Saturday: 1-5

The gallery was established in 1972 by Joseph A. Baird, Jr. Dr. Baird's scholarly background and interest in a wide variety of artistic areas has given the gallery a particular flavor and diversity, which underly its general emphasis on art in the United States.

California art from 1850 to 1940 is only one focus of the gallery's program. From the beginning, there have been exhibitions of period and modern work. The gallery has mounted several "rediscovery" retrospectives of figures of the recent past such as Martin Baer, Franz Bischoff, Ray Boynton, and Selden Connor Gile. Contemporary painters have also been shown.

In photography and the graphic arts, the 19th century has been emphasized. Dr. Baird and his assistant, Gary Carson, are available for special appointments to discuss the needs of collectors and corporations.

Antonio Jacobsen, *City of Savannah,* 22″ x 36″, oil on canvas. Smith Gallery (New York).

Thomas Birch, untitled, 27″ x 39″, oil on canvas. Schwarz Gallery (Philadelphia).

Old Print Gallery

Old Print Gallery 1212-31st St. NW, Washington, D.C. 20007
(202)965-3777 Monday-Saturday: 10-6

Specializing in original 18th and 19th-century American prints and maps, this decade-old Georgetown establishment is located just a few steps from busy M Street. It has a very large stock, which includes wood engravings by Winslow Homer and Thomas Nast taken from old *Harper's Weekly* magazines, and prints from other publications such as *Judge* and *Puck,* which published political cartoons.

Of major interest are prints from George Catlin's 1841 *North American Indian Portfolio* and Carl Bodmer's aquatints made to accompany Prince Maximilian's journal, *Travels in the Interior of North America* published in 1832-34.

Views of cities and landscapes taken from old books and newspapers from all over the world are numerous, as are historical prints from the Civil War. The varied stock of maps from the 16th through 19th centuries includes maps by the Blaeus, Visscher, DeWitt, Homann, Munster, Delisle, and other fine cartographers.

Natural history prints— flowers by Redoute from France and Robert Thornton from England, along with birds by America's Audubon—are also available. Proprietors are Judy and James Blakely.

The Old Print Shop

The Old Print Shop, Inc. 150 Lexington Ave., New York, NY 10016 (212) 683-3950 Monday-Saturday: 9-5 May-August: Monday-Friday: 9-5

Established in 1898, the gallery remains in its original location just above Gramercy Park and is now entering its third generation as a family enterprise. The main interest is in the 18th-century engravings of Dawkins, Revere, Doolittle, Porgis, and Savage and American 19th century works on paper by Wall, Hill Bennet, Mottran, Bingham, Havell, Frost, Cozzens, and Homer. Special attention has always been accorded to the work of Currier & Ives.

Another area of concentration is the work of John J. Audubon, both the original aquatint engravings of *Birds of America* executed from 1827 to 1838 by Robert Havell and later American productions by Bowen of Philadelphia and Bien of New York. Original Audubon prints in fine condition can be found in the antique bins.

The stock is arranged for quick reference by location for views and maps. Foreign, American, and other materials are arranged by subject matter. Areas covered are sporting subjects, natural history, botany, trades and industries, history, the West, yachts and steamers, naval and whaling subjects, politics and genre by the great artists, engravers, and lithographers of the past.

Pannonia

Pannonia Galleries 1043 Madison Ave., New York, NY 10021 (212) 628-1168 Monday-Friday: 11-5 or by appointment August: closed

Located in the heart of New York's art gallery world, this gallery offers traditional 19th century European paintings in an intimate setting. Paintings on exhibition, mainly oils from 1850 to 1920, change regularly. Selections include works from England, France, Spain, Italy, Denmark, Belgium, Holland, Austria, Germany, and Hungary. The main areas of focus are landscape, genre, animal, and floral paintings. All are framed and most paintings are signed and documented.

The gallery space is divided into two rooms. In the front gallery the special-ties are French figure, landscape, and floral paintings. Works on view are by

James Buttersworth, *Yacht Race,* (c. 1880), 9″ x 12″, oil on panel. Smith Gallery (New York).

Edward Potthast, *On the Beach,* 12″ x 15″, oil on panel. Ira Spanierman Gallery (New York).

such renowned artists as Adolphe Bouguereau, Camille Corot, Jules Dupre, and Charles Daubigny of the Barbizon school. Also displayed here are works by late 19th- and early 20th-century French artists Lebourg, Leon L'Hermitte, Louis Valtat and Gustave Dore. The back room is devoted to English landscape and animal paintings by artists such as John F. Herring, Henry John Boddington, the Williams family, Percy, Meadows, Landseer, and Cole. Occasionally, the gallery handles American 19th-century paintings and drawings.

Petersen   Petersen Galleries   270 N. Rodeo Dr., Beverly Hills, CA 90210   (213) 274-6705   Monday-Friday: 10-6, Saturday: 11-5 or by appointment

Important paintings by American artists are featured here. Works by American impressionist painters generally dating between 1870 and 1930 include major artists such as William Merritt Chase, Mary Cassatt, Childe Hassam, George Inness, Ernest Lawson, and John Sloan. Another area of specialization of the gallery is art by painters of the American West from about 1860 to 1930. Represented in the gallery are well-known artists such as Remington, Charles Russell, Henry Farny, F.T. Johnson, William R. Leigh, and O. Weighorst. California artists working in a regional sub-style of impressionism to 1930 are also represented. They include F. Bischoff, A. S. Clark, E. Payne, and W. Wendt. Also to be seen are paintings by the famous wildlife masters R. Bonheur, W. Kuhnert, E. Osthaus, P. Rousseau, and A. Barye. In addition to the regularly rotating exhibits, major retrospective exhibitions of an artist's estate are periodically featured and accompanied by illustrated catalogs.

Marilyn Pink   Marilyn Pink/Master Prints & Drawings   817 N. La Cienega Blvd., Los Angeles, CA 90069   (213) 657-5810   Monday-Friday: 12-5; Saturdays and other times by appointment

A small white house set in a garden down a driveway away from the busy La Cienega Blvd. houses an extraordinary collection of significant works of art on paper, drawings and prints of major artists and schools from the 15th through the mid-20th centuries. Both American and European artists are represented. One is likely to find first edition Audubon prints from the *Birds of America* and the *Viviparous Quadrupeds*, and Currier & Ives prints of various subjects. Also available are prints by well-known 19th- and 20th-century artists such as Julian Alden Weir, William Merritt Chase, Thomas Hart Benton, John Sloan, Rockwell Kent, Paul Landacre, John Steuart Curry, Mary Cassatt, and James A. McNeill Whistler. A special interest of the gallery is prints by early American modernists, including Louis Lozowick, Louis Schanker, Paul Kelpe, and Arthur Dove.

The gallery is notable for drawings by the old masters and the European masters. It has mounted one of the largest Pierre Bonnard drawing exhibitions seen in recent years. Vuillard drawings are a mainstay of the gallery, as are drawings and watercolors by impressionists, post-Impressionists, and other 19th- and early 20th-century French artists. The Russians are represented by the avant-garde works of Mikhail Larionov and Nathalie Gontcharova. Dance drawings are represented by Leon Bakst as well as set and costume designers of the early 20th century.

German artists represented are Kathe Kollwitz, Max Pechstein, Erik Heckel, Franz Marc, Oskar Kokoschka, and some of the German impressionists such as Lovis Corinth and Max Liebermann.

This is a gallery that is always innovative; it is especially dedicated to showing the thematic or stylistic relationship between drawings and prints.

Ammi Phillips, *Portrait of a Lady Holding her Glasses,* 30″x 24″, oil on canvas. Galerie St. Etienne (New York).

Redfern   Redfern Gallery   17310 Ventura Blvd., Encino, CA 91316   (213) 990-4269   Tuesday-Saturday: 10-6

The gallery features paintings by 19th- and 20th-century American impressionists. Among the major works shown here are animal paintings by Thomas B. Craig, snowscenes by Alfred Jansen, landscapes by impressionistic California artist Hansen Putoff, and figurative portraits and landscapes by Jean Mannheim. The gallery handles works by the Southern California school of plein air painters (1840-1900s) who formed the Laguna Beach Art Colony, such as Edgar Payne, William Went, Maurice Braun, and Joseph Kleitsch.

The gallery carries a fine selection of European artists as well. Works by Olivetti Morriety, Italian figurative artist who paints opaque watercolors of cathedrals, are always on hand as well as works by Frenchman Enjolaris, who paints interiors of women's boudoirs.

The rest of the gallery space has been set aside for the print works of major contemporary artists such as Marc Chagall, Joan Miro, Francisco Zuniga, and Norman Rockwell.

Schweitzer   Schweitzer Gallery   958 Madison Ave., New York, NY 10021   (212) 535-5430   Monday-Friday: 10-5:30

Fewer than 20 paintings are on view at any one time in this gallery. The bulk of the inventory is stored in bins according to size. American paintings on one wall feature 19th and 20th-century artists such as John Singer Sargent, George Inness, David Johnson, and Jerome Thompson. Also on view are some old masters and other artists of the period 1658 through 1720, such as Giovanni Cassana and Eugene Isabey.

The gallery also carries paintings from the French Barbizon school including Narcisse Diaz de la Pena, Camille Corot, the Dupre family and Rosa Bonheur, in addition to Italian painters such as the Induno brothers, T. Sighorini, T. Cremona, F. Zandomeneghi, A. Pasini, and G. Boldini. A unique feature of the gallery is an art library of 4000 volumes. Over 1000 illustrations and files are available to students and persons who qualify.

Frank S. Schwarz   Frank S. Schwarz and Son   1806 Chestnut St., Philadelphia, PA 19103 (215) 563-4887   Monday-Saturday: 10-5   July-August: closed Saturday

Established in 1930 in Atlantic City, New Jersey, the firm moved to its present location in 1940. Mr. Schwarz, who is semiretired, has turned the operation over to his son, who expanded the business to include a Main Line branch in suburban Ardmore. Although a variety of antiques is always available, the firm's specialty is 19th-century American and European paintings.

The main gallery features important groups of 19th-century paintings. European paintings include artists from England, Holland, France, Italy, Belgium, and Germany. American art may include works by William Merritt Chase, James Hamilton, Edmund Darch Lewis, and William Trost Richards.

American 18th-century silver has always been a prime interest of the gallery. The stock usually has some unique pieces of early silver as well as a selection of 19th-century American and English pieces. There are always examples of 18th-century tall clocks, commemorative medals, and china by Philadelphia porcelain-maker William Ellis Tucker.

Edward Hicks, *The Peaceable Kingdom* (1849), 24″ x 30″, oil on canvas.
Galerie St. Etienne (New York).

Henri-Joseph Harpignies, *La Seine a Paris* (1881), 7″ x 10″, watercolor. H. Terry-Engell (New York).

Smith

Smith Gallery   1045 Madison Ave., New York, NY 10021   (212) 744-6171
Monday-Saturday: 11-6 July: Monday-Friday: 10-5   August: Closed

This large gallery concentrates in several areas. It specialized in marine paintings of the nineteenth and early twentieth centuries, primarily American. These oil portraits of ships, notable for their historical value, are expertly painted by well-known artists C. S. Raleigh, Fred Pansing, James Bard and W. P. Stubbs, among others.

Contemporary artists Albert Nemethy and Keith Miller also paint marine subjects, which are carefully researched for historical accuracy. Miller's large watercolors portray America's Cup Race prior to 1910 and New York port scenes. Nemethy depicts in muted colors the Hudson River as it existed in the nineteenth century, complete with sidewheelers and scenery.

The gallery also features contemporary Western painters and sculptors. Among the painters is Don Troiani, a founding member of The Society of American Historical Artists (SAHA), whose military and historical figures from the 1840s to the 1880s are done with painstaking historical accuracy. Gregory Sumida, a protege of Andrew Wyeth, works in gouache, painting Indian encampments with a delicate touch. The gallery is the only East Coast representative of Harry Jackson, a foremost contemporary Western sculptor, whose standing figures and equestrian monuments in patinated and painted bronze are well known.

Unusual American folk sculpture from the nineteenth century is often featured. Weathervanes, tobacconist figures and ship models can be seen.

The gallery's calendar of exhibits reflects its various areas of specialization. The gallery features Western art in the fall, marine subjects from January through March, and a potpourri of exhibits, including folk sculpture, during the rest of the year.

Ira Spanierman

Ira Spanierman Gallery   50 East 78th St., New York, NY 10021   (212) 879-7085   Tuesday-Saturday: 9:30-5:30

For over 35 years this gallery has specialized in American paintings of the 19th and early 20th centuries. It is located a short walk from the Metropolitan and Whitney Museums.

The three major areas of specialization are the Hudson River school, luminism, and American impressionism. The gallery always has major paintings by at least one of the Hudson River school artists, such as John Frederick Kensett, Jasper F. Cropsey, Asher B. Durand, and Thomas Doughty. Among the most prominent luminists recently handled by the gallery are Martin Johnson Heade, S.R. Gifford, and Fitz Hugh Lane. The collection of American impressionists includes major works by John Singer Sargent, William Merritt Chase, Theodore Robinson, John Henry Twachtman, J. Alden Weir, and others.

Also handled by the gallery are important works by 19th-century artists of the West, such as Charles Bird King and Alfred Jacob Miller, as well as Frederic Remington, Charles M. Russell, and Henry Farny. Included in the collection are significant paintings by Taos School artists, such as Joseph H. Sharp and Ernest Blumenschien among others.

John H. Surovek

John H. Surovek Fine Arts, Inc.   337 Worth Ave., Palm Beach, FL 33480
(305) 832-0422   Monday-Friday: 9:30-5:30 and by appointment

The gallery is located on the grounds of Via Mizner, the late architect Addison Mizner's residence in Palm Beach. The company specializes in the acquisition and placement of fine 19thand 20th-century American drawings, watercolors, and paintings; although, on occasion, one might find European selections among the American works.

Henri Fantin-Latour, *Vase de Roses blanches* (1877), 18½″ x 17½″. oil on canvas.
H. Terry-Engell (New York).

Albert Le Bourge, *Le Quai de La Seine,* 15″ x 23″, oil on canvas. H. Terry Engell (New York).

The principal areas of concentration are American impressionism, with selected works by Childe Hassam, Maurice Prendergast, Ernest Albert, Abbott Fuller Graves, Frank Myer Boggs, Ernest Lawson, Jane Peterson, and Mary Cassatt. Another area with strong examples is American genre painting with selected works by such masters as Winslow Homer, John G. Brown, Andrew Wyeth, and E.L. Henry. A third and strong category of representation is Ash Can school works by Arthur B. Davies, John Sloan, Everett Shinn, Reginald Marsh, and George Luks. Additionally, there is a fine selection of drawings by many of the above named artists.

While the gallery does not concentrate in American printmaking, on occasion, and by request, the owners will make available certain master prints by John James Audubon, Edward Hopper, Louis Lozowick, and others.

St. Etienne

Galerie St. Etienne   24 W. 57th St., New York, NY 10019   (212) 245-6734   Tuesday-Saturday: 11-5   Summer: closed Saturday

The gallery, founded by the late Dr. Otto Kallir in 1939, has always specialized in early 20th-century Austrian and German expressionism as well as European and American naive art of the 19th and 20th centuries. About twice a year, comprehensive exhibitions are organized and accompanied by book-length, illustrated catalogues which explore the particular subject in depth. Though a commercial gallery, St. Etienne also functions as an educational resource; it maintains extensive archives which serve the scholar and serious collector as well as a wide public.

Egon Schiele, Oskar Kokoschka, Gustav Klimt, Alfred Kubin, Lovis Corinth, and Kaethe Kollwitz are among the now famous European artists this gallery has introduced to the United States. St. Etienne also introduced Anna Mary Robertson (Grandma) Moses, held her first one-woman show in 1940, and has represented her ever since. A large number of works by these artists is generally on view or available.

The gallery carries a full range of 19th- and 20th-century American folk art, including works by Edward Hicks and Ammi Phillips, as well as pieces by lesser-known and anonymous painters. In the area of European art, works by contemporaries of Klimt and Schiele, such as Jungnickel and Laske, are exhibited. The gallery also handles painter Richard Gerstl, an artist whose work is extremely rare and not often available. The gallery has sporadically devoted solo shows to such German artists as Lovis Corinth, Ernst Barlach, and Paula Modersohn-Becker.

The gallery has a collection of oils, watercolors, drawings, and prints by several lesser-known Austrian expressionists, such as Oskar Laske and L. H. Jungnickel; by the American expressionists Martin Pajeck and Marvin Meisels; and oils by the contemporary American folk artist Nan Phelps, in addition to works by other 19th and 20th century naive painters.

Maurice Sternberg

Galleries Maurice Sternberg   612 N. Michigan, Chicago, IL 60611   (312) 642-1700   Monday-Friday: 9-5, Saturday: 10-4

Located on the second floor, the spacious place is crowded with paintings, drawings, sculptures, and art objects, many which are of high quality. Director Sternberg travels around the world buying and selling work and dealing often with museum purchasers as well. Offering a wide variety of works that include numerous styles, historical periods, and ideas, Sternberg's space is clearly filled with riches. Though he is essentially interested in displaying 19th- and

Francis D. Millet, *The Mandolin Lesson* (c. 1884), 26″ x 29″, oil on canvas.
Richard York Gallery (New York).

Eugene Boudin, *Entre du Port de Saint-Valery* (1891), 14″ x 22″, oil on canvas. H. Terry-Engell Gallery (New York).

20th-century American and European artists, Sternberg seems to favor the work of the 20th-century impressionists.

Important paintings of the 19th century include masters of impressionist and genre schools, going into the early years of the 20th century and into the modern masters. An important part of the gallery is devoted to American Western art of the older painters and of the Taos school. Additionally, important works by Oscar Berninghaus have recently shown up at the gallery. Sternberg does not represent any experimental or avant-garde artists.

The work shown here ranges across a wide spectrum in both style and price. Other gallery artists included are Demetre Chiaparus, Pierre Le Faguays, Marcel Bouraine, and Jean Dupas.

Taggart & Jorgensen

Taggart & Jorgensen   3241 P Street NW, Washington, D.C. 20007   (202) 298-7676   Monday-Saturday: 11-5

The firm, which recently moved from Los Angeles, specializes in 19th- and early 20th-century American and European paintings and watercolors. Primary emphasis is placed on the Hudson River school of American landscape painting and luminism, as well as on American impressionism. In addition, a wide selection of English and continental paintings and watercolors is always in the gallery.

Among the American artists the gallery handles are Hudson River school artists William Trost Richards and Louis Remy Mignot; luminist William Bradford; impressionists Edward Redfield, Abbott Fuller Graves, William Merritt Chase, Daniel Garber, and Frank Boggs; still-life painter Severin Roesen; genre painter John George Brown; and 20th-century illustrator Norman Rockwell.

European artists represented include English Victorian painters Evelyn De Morgan, Benjamin W. Leader, and Atkinson Grimshaw; British illustrator Kate Greenaway; Barbizon school painter Leon Lhermitte; and French impressionists Eugene Boudin and Euguene Galien-Laloue.

H. Terry-Engell

H. Terry-Engell Gallery   22 East 76th St., New York, NY 10021   (212) 535-9800   Monday-Saturday: 10-6

Originally located in London where it opened in 1956, the gallery moved to New York in 1982, featuring 19th-century French paintings and watercolors. Impressionists, post-Impressionists, Barbizon school painters, and painters of the Paris school are all to be found.

The gallery consists of four sections. The first is the reception area where exhibitions are held. It is here that the gallery hosted its first exhibition, "Paris Visits New York—La Belle Epoque." A short corridor leads into the main room, which displays a selection of 19th-century French watercolors by artists such as J. F. Raffaelli and gouaches by Maurice Utrillo, as well as works by Jean Beraud, Antoine Vollon, Georges Michel, and S. Lepine.

Valley House

Valley House Gallery, Inc.   6616 Spring Valley Rd.   Dallas TX 75240 (214) 239-2441   Monday-Friday: 10-5; Saturday: 10-3

The gallery, founded by Donald and Margaret Vogel in 1953, is nestled in a five-acre garden in a residential area of north Dallas. Valley House was one of the first galleries to exhibit contemporary art in this region and now specializes in 19th- and early 20th-century European and American paintings, drawings, and prints.

John Frederick Peto, *Lantern, Books and Corn Cob Pipe,* 18″ x 13″ oil on academy board. Richard York Gallery (New York).

The estates of Hugh Breckenridge and Morgan Russell have been represented at the gallery with an important catalog published on Breckenridge. The contemporary artists represented are working in many media and styles, including abstract, figurative, and surrealistic. James Twitty and Gottfried Honegger work in abstract styles. Donald Vogel, Loren Mozley, and Fred Nagler work in a figurative manner. Hub Miller and Valton Tyler work in surrealistic styles.

A unique aspect of the gallery is the garden which is ideally suited to sculpture exhibition including Henry Moore, Sorel Etrog, Peter Chinni, Charles Umlauf, and Mike Cunningham.

There has been a recent emphasis on master printmakers due to Kevin Vogel's personal interest in prints and drawings. The gallery periodically arranges exhibitions of Whistler prints or shows of several artists with a theme.

The viewing room of the gallery houses a library which is being compiled for appraisal and research needs.

Richard York

Richard York Gallery   21 E. 65th St., New York, NY 10021   (212) 772-9155   Tuesday-Saturday: 10-5:30

Recently opened, the gallery shows an extensive array of 19th- and early 20th-century American painters with a range as broad as landscapes by Hudson River school painter Thomas Doughty from the 1830s to the modernist paintings of Ralston Crawford form the 1960s.

From the 19th century, featured works are still lifes by Levi Wells Prentice, Severin Roesen, and John Frederick Peto; genre paintings by Alfred Cornelius Howland, De Scott Evans, and Seymour Guy; Hudson River school landscapes by John Frederick Kensett, Sanford R. Gifford, Asher B. Durand, and James Hope; Western landscapes by Albert Bierstadt, Thomas Moran, Henry Farny, and Charles Wimar; and French Barbizon school paintings by George Inness, Homer Dodge Martin, and William Keith.

Of the 20th century, works from the Ash Can school are often available, including those by John Sloan, William Glackens, Everett Shinn, and George Luks. Works may also be found by some members of the Stieglitz group, including Charles Demuth, Georgia O'Keeffe, and Arthur Dove. Paintings by Oscar Bluemner, Elsie Driggs, and Charles Sheeler have also appeared in the gallery.

The gallery has given attention to work by female artists. One past exhibit featured works by Ellen Day Hale, a Bostonian impressionist painter who had earlier exhibited in the Paris salon.

The best

at the

Art Galleries

Thomas Eakins, *John A. Thorton*, 24″ x 20″, oil on canvas. Frank S. Schwarz & Son (Philadelphia).

Isaac Snowman, *A Small Bouquet* (c. 1885), 24″ x 36″, oil on canvas. James-Atkinson Gallery (Houston).

Paul Camille Guigou, *Laveuses au Bord de Riviera* (1867), 11½″ x 23¼″, oil on canvas. H. Terry-Engell Gallery (New York).

Frederick Carl Frieseke, *Windy Day at the Beach*, 55″ x 52″, oil on canvas.
David David Gallery (Philadelphia).

Frederick Carl Frieseke, *Afternoon Tea on the Terrace*, 55″ x 56″, oil on canvas.
David David Gallery (Philadelphia).

Daniel R. Knight, *Normandy Girl Sitting in Garden*, 32″ x 26″, oil on canvas. Daniel B. Grossman Fine Art (New York).

Enoch Wood Perry, *On Watch*, 24" x 20", oil on canvas. Jeffrey Alan Gallery (New York).

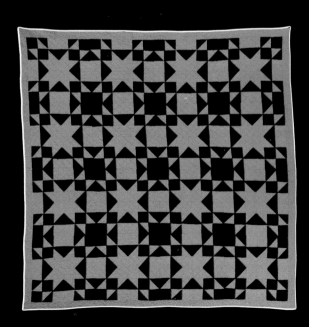

Ohio Amish Quilt, 78" x 78". Made in America (New York).

James E. Meadows, *Inn at Chiddingsford* (1878), 30″ x 51″, oil on canvas. James-Atkinson Gallery (Houston).

James Bard, *The Brother Jonathon* (1851), 32″ x 52″, oil on canvas. Smith Gallery (New York).

Cesare A. Detti, *Market Day*, 30½" x 41", oil on canvas. Daniel B. Grossman Fine Art. (New York).

John Frederick Peto, *Violin, fan and Books* (1880), 9½" x 13½", oil on canvas. David David Gallery (Philadelphia).

John Singleton Copley, *Jabez Bowen*, 29″ x 24″, oil on canvas. Kennedy Galleries (New York).

Evert Pieters, *On the Shore*, 35" x 47", oil on canvas. Pannonia Galleries/Lisa Schiller Fine Art. (New York).

Camille Pissarro, *Paysage de l'Oise a Pontoise* (1876), 15" x 22", oil on canvas. H. Terry-Engell Gallery (New York).

Asian &
Oriental
Galleries

Asian & Oriental Galleries

By Location

California
San Francisco:
  Ashkenazie
Georgia
Atlanta:
  The Gables
New York
New York City:
  Caro
  Chait
  Fil Caravan
  Weisbrod & Dy
Washington DC
  Shogun
  Trocadero

By Specializations

Asian Sculpture:
  Trocadero
Chinese Antiques and Porcelain:
  Caro
  Chait
  The Gables
  Trocadero
  Weisbrod & Dy
Islamic Art:
  Fil Caravan
Jade Carvings:
  Ashkenazie
  Chait
  Weisbrod & Dy
Prints:
  Shogun

Ashkenazie & Co.   950 Mason St., San Francisco, CA 94108   (415) 391-3440   Monday-Friday: 10-6; Saturday: 10-5   *Ashkenazie*

Tucked away in the lobby of the Fairmont Hotel at the top of Nob Hill is this unusual gallery specializing in jade carvings of museum quality. The age of the inventory ranges from the Han period (206 B.C.-220 A.D.) through the 19th century. The stock contains 300 pieces consisting mainly of carvings, vases, and figures, both large and small. Chinese ivory carvings can also be found.

   The gallery handles a large selection of Japanese inro (a small case for carrying small objects worn on the girdle of a kimono). The inro is held in place by a netsuke which is carried here as well. Netsukes can be ivory or wooden figures carved in the images of plants, fruits, animals or legendary or human figures. Most of the inro here is lacquer, the purse of the upper class.

   Not to be missed are the massive 18th- and 19th-century Japanese bronze figures.

Frank Caro Gallery   41 E. 57th St., New York, NY 10022   (212) 753-2166   *Frank Caro*
Tuesday-Saturday: 9-4:30   late August: closed

Formerly called the C. T. Loo Gallery, the Frank Caro Gallery has been in its present location on the second floor of the art deco Fuller Building since 1929. Specializing in fine Chinese antiques, the gallery also displays the ancient arts of India and Southeast Asia. Some very important early Indian stone and bronze figures line the long entrance gallery. In the back galleries there are rare and beautiful Chinese ceramics and jades displayed in glass cases and interspersed with hanging scroll paintings by old Chinese masters.

   Mr. Caro appreciates early Chinese ceramics, which predate the 8th century A.D., and simple but elegant Ming period rosewood furniture, which is usually distributed throughout the galleries. There is almost always an important early Buddhist stone or bronze sculpture on exhibition.

   More numerous are the porcelain wares of the Sung, Ming, and Ch'ing dynasties displayed in cases. Some of the display cases are devoted to exhibiting terra cotta figures and vessels of the Han and T'ang dynasties as well as the very early vessels and implements of Bronze Age China.

   Special exhibitions are held on the average of one a year. Some of the past ones have included important Sung, Ming, and Ch'ing paintings, contemporary

123

Chinese paintings and calligraphy, and Ming period furniture. Planned for the future is an exhibition of rare Buddhist bronze and stone sculpture from China, Thailand, and Cambodia.

Ralph M. Chait

Ralph M. Chait Galleries, Inc.   12 East 56th St., New York, NY 10022
(212) 758-0937   Monday-Saturday: 10-5:30   Summer: Monday-Friday: 10-5:30

The gallery, which has been in business since 1910, is presently carried on by Allan S. Chait and Marion Chait Howe, children of the founder. The Chaits provide a history of fine Chinese porcelain and pottery and travel to China to collect 95% of their inventory. The showroom includes a range of large and small Chinese artifacts. An example is an imperial famille rose peach vase of the Yung Cheng period (1723-35). Famille rose is a style of Chinese porcelain in which the decoration is named after a prominent pink rose. Also exhibited are carvings of the T'ang period (618-906), a golden age in Chinese art, and groupings of K'ang Hsi period (1662-1722) porcelain, including pieces of that period of famille verte in which the decoration is dominated by various greens. To be seen also are Wan Li wood and lacquer images. Another feature of the gallery is 18th and 19th century Chinese export silver including all forms.

Opposite: Chinese Porcelain figure. Ralph M. Chait Galleries (New York).

The gallery boasts a fine library on Oriental art. Part of the collection is stored in the basement of the gallery, which also houses a private laboratory installed for testing the precise age of the antiques.

Fil Caravan

Fil Caravan, Inc.   1050 Second Ave., New York, NY 10022   (212) 421-5972   Daily: 12-6

These dealers in Islamic Art are located in the heart of the East Side shopping district of New York City. Established in 1976, the gallery serves an international clientele in all aspects of Islamic Art collecting, including antiques, jewelry, textiles, and rugs.

Middle Eastern metal arts comprise a wide range of decorative copper and brass articles of nomadic origin as well as silver and gold items from palaces. Fil Caravan has furnished large and decorative brass samovars to the Russian Tea Room in New York City. Unusual scientific instruments, such as an early 18th-century astrolabe, are among the more important objects offered. Silver and gold inlaid vessels, boxes, and weapons are displayed with ancient bronzes and other metal objects.

The gallery has a fine selection of fine Caucasian rugs, kilims, and other oriental rugs and textiles.

Jewelry selections include antique silver belts, necklaces, and rare rings from throughout the Middle East. A high-quality selection of amber jewelry with antique and recent examples is also displayed.

Gables

The Gables   3125 Piedmont Rd., NE, Atlanta, GA 30305   (404) 231-0734
Monday-Saturday: 10-5:30

The Gables is a family owned and operated corporation and has been in business for five years in a renovated Victorian home in the heart of Buckhead, a shopping area in Atlanta. The gallery specializes in antique Chinese porcelain imported directly from China, and imported country French and English furniture, porcelain, and carpets. One of the owners travels to Europe and China frequently and personally selects all the merchandise with great care. The antique Chinese porcelain ranges from 50 to 150 years old. The

Chinese government will not allow export of anything over 150 years. The country French furniture is predominantly 18th and 19th century with emphasis in armoires, buffets, chairs, and tables. The gallery receives shipments 4 times a year from France. The Gables also carries many English and Irish pine pieces. The porcelain department is constantly expanding, as the owners are importing more and more 18th and 19th century Chinese export pieces from Europe, in addition to Imari ware (Japanese porcelain characterized by soft shades of green, blue, yellow, and orange), rose medallion ware (Chinese porcelain with medallions of people, flowers, birds, and butterflies), and blue willow (Chinese porcelain of white and blue).

Shogun

Shogun Gallery   1083 Wisconsin Ave., NW, Washington, D.C.   (202) 965-5454   Monday-Sunday: 11-6

This Georgetown gallery specializes in Japanese woodblock prints from the 18th century to the present. Emphasis is on 19th-century Ukiyo-e prints and the so-called transitional period from 1912 to 50, when woodblock prints were still very traditional in style, but began to incorporate Western perspective and modeling.

Among the better-known names represented in this large stock are the 18th-century master Utamaro, and 19th-century artists Hokusai, Hiroshige, and Yoshitoshi. Two of the finest landscape artists from the transitional period are Hiroshi Yoshida and Kawase Hasui, named a national living treasure by the Japanese government in 1956. Among the leading contemporary woodblock artists are Yoshitosha Mori, Jun'Ichiro Sekino, and Toshi Yoshida, among numerous others.

Gallery owner Toni Liberthson is a longtime collector and was a private dealer in New York before opening Shogun Gallery in 1978. Books on Japanese woodblock prints, as well as many posters, are also on sale.

Trocadero

Trocadero Asian Art   1501 Connecticut Ave., NW, Washington, DC, 20036   (202) 234-5656   Tuesday-Saturday: 10:30-6:30

Opposite: Head of Buddah, Chi Dynasty (6th century, China), 14½″ high, Limestone. Weisbrod & Dy (New York).

Located in the center of Washington D.C. on Dupont Circle, the gallery specializes in Asian sculpture and fine Chinese porcelain. Ming (1367-1644) and Ching (1644-1912) porcelain are well represented. Indian stone sculpture from the 2nd through the 12th centuries and Chinese bronzes from the 13th century B.C. through the 16th century are widely handled. Also on exhibition are 14th through 18th-century Himalayan bronze sculpture and ritual objects.

Chinese furniture is another major area of specialization. Fine 16th and 17th-century pieces of Huang Huali wood and 18th and 19th-century Hungmu pieces are available ranging from desks, altar tables, and chairs to large cabinets. The works of art are well displayed with an abundance of natural lighting. It is not unusual to find objects such as Japanese lacquer and sculpture, ivory, wood carvings, cloisonne jade, and rhinoceros horn from Southeast Asia.

Weisbrod & Dy

Weisbrod & Dy Ltd.   906 Madison Ave., New York, NY 10021   (212) 734-6350   Monday-Saturday: 10-5

The gallery specializes in a broad range of high-quality Chinese works of art from ancient times to the early 18th century (2500 B.C.-1820). Ceramic figures from the T'ang dynasty (618-906) and bronze vessels from the Sung and Chou dynasties are featured. The Sung dynasty (960-1290) which produced fine

stoneware is represented in the gallery by a selection of ceramic bowls and vases. Jade figurines and vessels are shown dating from the archaic period to the 18th century. The Ming dynasty (1367-1644) and Qing dynasty (1644-1912) both produced cloisonne enamelware such as the incense burners, vases, and vessels on display. Not to be overlooked are bowls and bottles of Chinese glass exhibiting many techniques such as overlay glass with many colors as well as Imperial monochrome.

Mr. Weisbrod maintains a fine group of Chinese furniture. Among the collection are tables, some of which are lacquered and chairs and stands from the 16th century through the 19th century. There is also a strong interest in Chinese wood sculpture from all periods.

Archaic vessel and cover, *Yu,* Shang Dynasty, 10″ high, bronze. Weisbrod & Dy (New York).

Eclectic
Galleries

Eclectic Galleries

By Location

California
San Francisco:
    Therien
Santa Barbara:
    Breitweiser-Studio 2
Connecticut
Canton:
    Jenkins
Lisban:
    Blum
Massachusetts
Boston:
    Shreve, Crump & Low
New Mexico
Albuquerque:
    Ozark's
Santa Fe:
    Tara
New York
New York City:
    America Hurrah
    Blumka
    Ricco-Johnson
    Made in America
    Newhouse
    Rosenberg & Stiebel
    Schoellkopf
    Stair
    Stephenson
    Woodard
South Carolina
Charleston:
    Austin
Texas
Dallas:
    Investors
Fort Worth:
    Sundance

By Specializations

Americana:
    America Hurrah
    Blum
    Ricco-Johnson
    Made in America
    Ozark's
    Schoellkopf
    Sundance
    Tara
    Woodard
Cabinets, Objects:
    Jenkins
    Rosenberg & Stiebel
Glass & Porcelain:
    Shreve, Crump & Low
    Stair
Mirrors:
    Stephenson
    Therien
Prints & Paintings:
    Breitweiser-Studio 2
    Investors
    Newhouse
    Rosenberg & Stiebel
Renaissance Art:
    Blumka
    Rosenberg & Stiebel
Silver:
    Austin
    Breitweiser-Studio 2
    Jenkins
    Shreve, Crump & Low
Varieties:
    Rosenberg & Stiebel
    Schoellkopf
    Shreve, Crump & Low
    Stephenson
    Therien

America Hurrah   766 Madison Ave., New York, NY 10021   (212) 535-1930

Tuesday-Saturday: 11-6

Located on the 2nd and 3rd floors of a 19th-century brownstone, this gallery has specialized in American antique quilts and American folk art for the last 15 years. In addition to quilts, there are 19th-century textiles including hooked rugs, yarn-sewn rugs, samplers, blankets, and coverlets. There is also a large inventory of American folk art, mostly 19th-century weathervanes, decoys, and carvings. A large selection of American primitive paintings is shown on the third floor. The collection includes works by Ammi Phillips, Noah North, Aschel Powers, William Mathew Prior, Joseph Davis, and Charles Hofmann and many anonymous folk paintings and watercolors.

Throughout the gallery there are fine examples of painted and decorated American country furniture. Blanket chests, cupboards, dressing tables, chairs, stools, and benches are also displayed. In addition, the gallery is filled with decorative country accessories such as baskets, wooden pottery, stoneware and spongeware.

Elizabeth Austin, Inc.   165 King St., Charleston, SC 29401   (803) 722-8227

Monday-Friday; 10-5 or by appointment

Located on a historic street, the shop concentrates primarily on American and English silver, although American furniture is also shown. Featured pieces of early American silver include the work of noted Boston silversmith Jacob Hurd, dating 1744. Early 18thand 19th-century hollowware and flatware are given prominence throughout the shop. Early Charles II salt trenchers (flat-based, glass-lined silver salt cellars) are highlighted in the English silver section of the collection.

Throughout the shop are pieces of 18thand 19th-century American furniture, including a Philadelphia double banquet table with marlboro legs (straight, grooved legs with a block as a foot), dating 1770-90; a Philadelphia piecrust table (a round-topped pedestal table with the narrow rim boldly scalloped like the crimped edge of a pie); a Federal-period (1790-1820) card table; and a signed American Sheraton-style dresser. There are also several Southern pieces, including a set of eight chairs with inlay dating 1790.

Displayed throughout the gallery are 19thand early 20th-century paintings. They include canvases by such well-known artists as 19th-century painter John W.

Pieced quilt, *Blazing Star and Compass* (c. 1845, New England). America Hurrah (New York).

Pieced quilt, *Broken Star.* Made in America (New York).

Twachtman, who was strongly influenced by French impressionism in his works depicting familiar scenes; and 20th-century artist Andrew Wyeth, who painted people and nature in a sparse, sharp-focus, realistic technique.

Jerome W. Blum

Jerome W. Blum   Ross Hill Rd., Lisban, CN 06351   (203) 376-0300   By appointment.

This gallery is located in a two-story National Trust house dating from about 1740 with the latest addition done in 1797. American and country 18th-century furniture is displayed on two floors. The first floor is set up as a living room completely equipped with a Chippendale dining table, Queen Anne chairs, and a sideboard. Scattered throughout is assorted pottery pieces, such as plates, pitchers, early slipware, Dutch delft and English delftware, Worcester and creamware.

The second floor concentrates on folk art and country furniture of the 18th and 19th centuries. There are various country pieces such as chests and tables in pine, maple, cherry, and mahogany. Also on this floor is a selection of miniature chests, tables, and chairs. Among the pieces of furniture, folk art is displayed in the form of weathervanes, carvings, decoys, baskets, and textiles and samplers from the New England area.

Another feature of the gallery is the Keeping Room, in which furniture and accessories relating to the hearth are found. There are hutches, tables, and chairs from the Hudson Valley as well as a selection of Queen Anne items. All types of fireplace equipment such as tools, screens, and andirons are also found here.

Blumka

Blumka Gallery   949 Park Ave., New York, NY 10028, (212) 734-3222   Monday-Friday: 10:30-5

The gallery is a fourth generation antique shop which originated in Vienna, Austria, and is now run by Mrs. Ruth Blumka and her daughter, Victoria Blumka-Nasatir. It specializes in medieval and Renaissance art, including sculpture, furniture and jewelry in a variety of styles. The objects are of various media, such as bronze, wood, marble, and stone. One can find 16th-century Renaissance bronzes by Italian artists such as Riccio, Vittorio and, later, Tacca. Also on display is terra-cotta sculpture from the school of Verrochio and a Madonna by Torrigianno. Medieval leather boxes as well as 16th-century jewels are shown as well as goldsmith works from Dresden.

There are several pieces of furniture at the gallery, including Italian Renaissance cassone chests. Also displayed are several Henry II cabinets with engraved decorations and 17th-century Dutch inlaid tables and chairs.

The gallery also deals in antique textiles, church vestments, and copes (semicircular mantles worn by priests) in warm velvets, brocades, and rich silks. There is also some emphasis on drawings with a special interest in drawings of objects.

Breitweiser-Studio 2

Breitweiser-Studio 2   11 E. dela Guerra, Santa Barbara, CA 93101   (805) 965-8100   Monday-Saturday: 11-5

The gallery recently moved to the historic dela Guerra adobe in the El Paseo. Featuring fine arts and antiques, Breitweiser has long specialized in California painters and sculptors working before 1940. Over 500 works include major paintings by such artists as Thomas Hill, Frederick Schafer, Hanson Puthuff, William Wendt, John Gamble, and Conrad Buff. Beyond the California

Floral applique quilt (c. 1860). America Hurrah (New York).

category are works by Hudson River school artist Thomas Doughty, Mary Cassatt and Alexander Archipenko.

The gallery also features a selection of Georgian and continental silver, and American silver including examples of Gorham from Providence, Rhode Island. Also displayed are English and American furniture and accessories, including carriage clocks (traveling clocks with handles), and bracket clocks (portable clocks, only occasionally found with a bracket). Faberge enamel desk clocks by master craftsman Hendrick Wigstrom are displayed as well.

Investors

The Investors Gallery   2901 Routh, Dallas, TX 75201   (214) 748-7831 Monday-Friday: 9-5

For over five years, the gallery has offered hard-to-find prints and paintings. The owners specialize in business memorabilia including a vast selection of antique stock certificates noted by the Los Angeles Times, sports collectibles ranging from college athletic cigarette silks to antique golf and tennis prints, and the engravings and lithographs of John J. Audubon. Special creativity and care is evident in the framed pieces. One can find antique golf clubs framed with a print and map of famed Scottish courses, and antique stock certificates framed with a picture of the company founder or a company advertisement. In addition to these areas of specialty, the gallery has a fine collection of English hunting prints, original Currier and Ives chromolithographs, American folk art and antique quilts, advertisement posters and signs, and old Texas and regional maps.

While the predominant focus is on prints and paintings, a limited amount of antique furniture from Windsor chairs to English writing desks is also offered at the gallery.

Richard H. Jenkins

Richard H. Jenkins   P.O. Box 448, Canton, CN 06019   (203) 693-8968   By appointment.

Prior to founding the firm nearly a decade ago, Richard Jenkins had long collected smaller antique objects of vertu of all provenances, bringing to the business a varied inventory of many periods and many places. English and American pieces are featured, but also included are items from Europe, Russia, China, Japan, and other eastern countries. The firm is dedicated to maintaining a large, diverse inventory of cabinet objects

Fine English silver smallwork is a specialty. Among the forms always well represented are snuff boxes and mulls (Scottish snuff boxes), vinaigrettes, nutmeg graters, patch boxes, counter boxes, pomanders, and etuis (small, flat, decorated cases to contain small items). All prominent known makers from Thomas Kedder and Simon Van de Passe through Nathanial Mills and Mathew Linwood to Sampson Mordan are apt to be well represented. Individual pieces of major importance are usually displayed. Gold objects and those of materials lesser than silver (iron, brass, wood, ivory, and porcelain) are always shown as well.

Chinese export small silverwork for the American and European markets is always present as are China trade objects in carved ivory and wood. American smallwork in all materials is a special interest limited only by its general scarcity. Oriental cabinet objects of all periods are well represented in all materials and forms. Pocket instruments and tools, including medical items, are among the more esoteric specializations of the firm. Sewing objects (other than thimbles) of unusual nature are always in stock in good quantity.

Stag Weathervane (late 19th century), 23″ high, painted wood. Ricco-Johnson Gallery (New York).

Two drawer blanket chest (1675-1690, Hartford County, C.T.). Ricco-Johnson Gallery (New York).

Art nouveau is among the more recent periods represented, especially in metal items of silver, gold, and bronze. Nineteenth century jewelry through art nouveau is a field of growing interest and is always shown. Emphasis is placed on periodic acqustions of Dutch, South German, French, Austrian, and Russian work of quality, limited only by its availability.

Ricco-Johnson

Ricco Johnson Gallery   475 Broome St., New York, NY 10013   (212) 966-0541   Tuesday-Saturday: 11-6

Set in New York's historic Cast Iron District, a former metal machine shop was transformed to showcase the American art form. The gallery carries works which span the centuries as well as a range of materials. Pieces predating 1880 are in ample supply, however, a selection of contemporary work is also displayed. The exhibit constantly changes, but one can always see rare examples of 17th-century Pilgrim furniture (the earliest New England Colonial furniture), kinetic whirligigs, primitive tools as decorative objects, and promotional display objects. Figures, fanciful sculpture and furniture in twig, grain-painted wood and carved wood, Menonnite and Amish quilts, and hand-hooked rugs, paintings, and weathervanes are also regularly available.

The owners regularly comb the United States for new sources of antiques, objects of vertu (fine art objects), as well as undiscovered talent. Folk artists are typically unschooled craftspeople who work independently without the influence of contemporary art styles.

The gallery is a work of art itself. Designer Lawrence Shapiro created new life in the landmark building where art can be seen on many levels with niches and private viewing areas that escort the viewer through several different environments.

Made in America

Made in America   1234 Madison Ave., New York, NY 10028   (212) 289-1113   Monday-Friday: 10:30-6; Saturday: 11-5:30

The gallery's emphasis is on varied and high-quality antique American quilts. Bed quilts, Amish quilts, crib quilts and others can be found here. The main concentration is on country items, which include pottery, paintings, hooked rugs, rag rugs and runners, fold toys and dolls, all reflecting America's rural past. Also on hand is *American Folk Dolls* by Wendy Lavitt, a partner in the shops. The book covers Black, Amish, Indian, and many other kinds of dolls. Gameboards, baskets, and mirrors are also carried. Pottery on display includes yellow ware (tableware with a brown glaze), sponged ware (household pottery on which color was applied by dabbing the surface with a sponge) and mocha pottery (pottery with bands of pigmented decoration applied while it was on the wheel). Baby dishes and plates are on hand.

Paintings in the gallery include 19th-century folk portraits, landscapes, and animal scenes. Folk sculpture includes portraits in wood, weathervanes, and sculptural toys.

Newhouse

Newhouse Galleries   19 East 66th St., New York, NY 10021   (212) 879-2700   Monday-Friday: 9:30-5

Now 104 years old, and in their third generation, the gallery has sold important paintings to American and European museums and distinguished private collectors. The gallery features fine old master paintings, beginning with the 14th-century Italian masters and including 16th and 17th-century Dutch and Flemish masters as well as 18th-century French and English masters. Artists

Miniature cupboard (19th century, New York State), 60″ high, painted wood.
Made in America (New York).

139

represented include Bernardino Luini, Jacopo di Cione, Rembrandt, Frans Hals, Anthony van Dyck, Peter Paul Rubens, Thomas Gainsborough, Thomas Lawrence, Joshua Reynolds, Canaletto, and Francesco Guardi.

On display are early Italian paintings, works by 17th-century Dutch and Flemish artists from the lesser masters through Rubens and Van Dyck, and paintings by 18th-century English portraitists Gainsborough and Henry Raeburn. American painters shown include the Peale family and impressionists Childe Hassam and William Merritt Chase.

There are representatives of the French Barbizon school, such as Camille Corot and Charles Daubigny as well as French impressionists, including Pierre Auguste Renoir, Alfred Sisley, Camille Pissarro, and Eugene Boudin.

The gallery has recently expressed a strong interest in Western Americana, including artists such as Charles Russell and Frederic Remington.

Ozark's

Ozark's Inc., and Tara Antiques, Inc.,   9450 Candelaria, NE Albuquerque, NM 87112   607 Old Santa Fe Trail, Santa Fe, NM 87501   (505) 293-3607/984-0623   Monday-Friday: 10-5, Saturday: 11-3

Both galleries specialize in 18th and 19-century American country furnishings and folk art, including graphic quilts, works from the Shaker and Amish sects, decorated stoneware, and baskets. Tara, a sister operation to Ozark's, is housed in a 150-year-old historic adobe dwelling. Both shops are reminiscent of the 18th- and 19th-centuries, housing pine, cherry, and walnut country furnishings from the New England area, and graphic quilts including some rare Amish geometric examples. One can find an 18th-century pine and chestnut setties with a curved back hailing from Maine, coupled with an early cobbler's bench that is suitable for a coffee table. The shop has a fine selection of Amish quilts that hang invitingly on the walls amid the offerings of country furnishings and accessories.

Rosenberg & Stiebel

Rosenberg & Stiebel, Inc.   32 East 57th St., New York, NY 10022   (212) 753-4368/888-5007   Monday-Friday: 10-5

Founded in Frankfurt, Germany, over 100 years ago, Rosenberg & Stiebel has been located in New York since 1939. A family concern operated by Eric Stiebel and his son Gerald, the gallery deals primarily in old master paintings and drawings, French 18th-century furniture, continental ceramics, and medieval and Renaissance art.

The reception room at Rosenberg & Stiebel is graced by an unusual 18th-century Dutch marquetry table with porcelain plaques and plates, an art nouveau regulateur, two Renaissance cabinets, a Regence prie-dieu, and two Renaissance candelabra which flank a Louis XVI lacquer music stand. Important European bronzes which date from the 16th century through the 18th century are concealed in the rear of the room.

The following two rooms are devoted primarily to the French 18th-century furniture for which Rosenberg & Stiebel is renowned. The pieces range from the period of Louis XIV to that of the Empire and are largely by important ebenistes and menuisiers such as Bernard van Risenburgh, Roentgen, Avisse, Demoulin, and Jacob. The other decorative objects displayed, including ormolu-mounted celadon urns, black laquered Japanese boxes, marquetry bellows, and bronze dore appliques also lay witness to the extreme luxury and impeccable craftsmanship of the 18th century. A small but exquisite selection of 18th-centuries Meissen and Sevres porcelain can be found in the side vitrines of the first of these rooms.

Cast-iron dog (late 19th century), 23″ high. Ricco-Johnson Gallery (New York).

Horse Weathervane (late 19th century, Maine), 20″ high, wood with sheet metal.
Ricco-Johnson Gallery (New York).

Clients may view old master paintings in an adjacent room. Very few works are permanently installed. Some are kept behind curtains but the majority are pulled from bins and displayed on easels for the potential buyer. The gallery concentrates mainly on French and Italian paintings and drawings of the 16th through the 19th centuries with masters such as Drouais, Jeaurat, Parmigianino, Pater, Tiepolo, and Vernet represented.

George E. Schoellkopf

George E. Schoellkopf   1065 Madison Ave., New York, NY 10028   (212) 879-3672   Tuesday-Thursday & Saturday: 10-5   Closed August

Those interested in seeing how American homes of yesteryear are furnished will want to visit this gallery which is on the block immediately east of the Metropolitan Museum. Schoellkopf has amassed one of the most complete selections of Americana on today's market with a very broad range of country furniture, folk art, quilts and weathervanes.

Among the furniture, the best offerings are the hard-to-find painted country furniture dating from the 18th and 19th centuries. The best pieces are those which have the original paint; some, but not all, are among the many pieces for sale. Rarely is it possible to identify the makers and often the anonymous pieces are the best crafted. One maker in particular did sign this work, E. B. Tracy, and Schoellkopf seeks out and often finds his works. Painted pieces are almost always made of native wood including maple, cherry, birch, pine and Pennsylvania walnut.

A lesser emphasis at the gallery—due to its unavailability—is what Schoellkopf refers to as "high country furniture". These pieces are very formal looking, somewhat resembling English pieces of the 18th century. Though some pieces are made of pine, the wood is often part of the aesthetic appeal, especially those pieces crafted from cherry and native tiger maple.

Paintings are also to be found which date from the late 18th to the early 19th centuries. Most are anonymous and are almost invariably either portraits or landscapes. Occasionally Schoellkopf will obtain works by some of the most recognized names in folk painting such as Ammi Phillips, Erastus Salisbury or those of the Prior-Hamblen Group.

Shreve, Crump and Low

Shreve, Crump and Low, Inc.   330 Boylston St., Boston, MA 02116   (617) 267-9100   Monday-Friday: 9:30-5; Saturday: 9:30-5   July & August: Monday-Friday: 9:30-5

Located near the Boston Public Gardens, the gallery began as a small shop on downtown Marlborough Street just before 1800. The founder, John McFarlane, was a jeweler, watchmaker, and silversmith. Through a series of partnerships, his shop has evolved to be Shreve, Crump and Low, Inc. Mr. Crump, who joined the firm in 1869, made frequent trips to Europe to purchase rich furnishings and art objects for his customers. This was the begining of Shreve's second floor Antiques Department.

The department is known for carrying English andsAmerican furniture and decorative arts as well as Chinese export porcelain. Glass, silver, porcelain, and prints of the late 18th century to 1830 are represented. English Chippendale, Hepplewhite, and Sheraton as well as American Federal period furniture are arranged in displays reflecting elegant rooms in a house. Glass, silver, and porcelain are placed in cases. Waterford, Sandwich, and English glass, English porcelain from Worcester, Derby, Chelsea, and Minton factories, and Staffordshire and Leeds earthenware are all represented. Fine English silver pieces in many forms by such makers as Thomas Whipham, Hester Bateman, William Chawner,

Jean-Antoine Houdin, *Bust of Thomas Jefferson* (1789), 28″ high, plaster. Rosenberg & Stiebel (New York).

and Paul Storrs are usually available. Chinese export porcelain, silver, and occasionally export furniture are also represented. The selection of prints concentrates on English hunting and sporting prints by Herring, Alkin, and Stubbs, late 18th-century marine engravings, and contemporary collotypes by Derek Gardner, Charles Vickery, and Montague Dawson. Floral prints by such artists as Jean-Baptiste Monnoyer and Dr. Thornton are sometimes available.

Stair & Co.

Stair & Co., Inc.   59 East 57th St., New York, NY 10022   (212) 355-7620
Monday-Saturday: 9:30-5:30   July and August: Monday-Friday: 9:30-5:30

The firm was simultaneously founded in 1912 in London and New York and their subsidiary company, Stair's Incurable Collector, started business in 1964. The galleries specialize in fine English 18th-century furniture and Chinese export porcelain. Stair's Incurable Collector specializes in sporting paintings and Regency furniture (an English furniture style in the early 19th century during the Regency of George IV).

The main specialty is 18th-century dining room furniture. In stock at all times are several dining room tables to seat from 8 to 18 people, a large collection of sideboards, and several sets of 18th-century dining room chairs, which are becoming increasingly hard to find.

Important pieces of furniture are carried in stock at all times. At present there is a suite of furniture with the label of Giles Grendey, a pair of rare padouk wood mirrors dating about 1730, and a superb Chippendale commode with serpentine front and carved cabriole legs.

Another feature of the gallery is the Georgian room which contains less elaborate, simpler pieces of furniture.

Garrick C. Stephenson

Garrick C. Stephenson   50 East 57th St., New York, NY 10022   (212) 753-2570   Monday-Friday: 10-5

Stephenson specializes in fine French furniture of the 18th and 19th centuries and is equally known for Chinese and Japanese lacquer furniture of the 17th, 18th, and 19th centuries.

Among current items on display are a Louis XVI mahogany and gilt bronze console desserte, a Louis XVI mahogany, ebony, and gilt bronze tric-trac table (for playing backgammon) inlaid with ivory, a transitional Louis XV/XVI lacquer commode with polychrome decorations, and a pair of Louis XVI mahogany etageres.

An early 18th-century Chinese black lacquer long table with exceptionally fine polychrome decorations, a pair of Ch'ien Lung dark brown lacquer side chairs with mother of pearl and polychrome decorations, and an 18th-century Japanese black lacquer low table are also displayed.

Always available is an unusual selection of mirrors, such as a Venetian mirror of the late 18th century and a Louis XIV mirror with a parquetry (geometric wood inlay) frame.

Pieces from other periods are represented. They include a late 18th century Russian rosewood commode inlaid with brass, a pair of English pine tall cabinets dating about 1770, and an Anglo-Indian commode in coromandel wood, inlaid with ivory, about 1820.

There are objects of art throughout, such as a pair of Louis XVI ormolu candlesticks, Canton enamelware, Chinese and Japanese porcelain and lacquer vases and lacquer boxes.

M.C. Kramer, Louis XVI console, mahogany and gilt bronze. Garrick C. Stephenson (New York).

Sundance Gallery   310 Main, Fort Worth, TX 76102   (817) 870-1001
Monday-Saturday: 10-5

The gallery is Dallas-Fort Worth's first folk art gallery. The 19th and early 20th century Americana include domestic objects such as quilts and bowls, ornamentation from homes, barns, shops, and boats, and objets d'art such as folk sculpture and ceramics.

As in most folk art, many of the artists are unknown, leaving the works to be judged on their creativity, their unique juxtaposition of utility and visual interest, and their rarity of craftsmanship. Represented in the gallery are folk sculptors David Alvarez and Felipe Archuleta of New Mexico. Also to be found is a complete series of Amsterdam edition *Birds of America* by Audubon.

Most of the folk art originated in the Northeast or in the Southwest, especially Texas and New Mexico, and reflects regional habits. From the Northeast are whirligigs, chests, carved signs and symbols, and 1870 weathervanes; from the Southwest, quilts, pottery, carved animals, belts, jewelry, and kitchen items.

Two or three special shows are held each year. Special exhibits of folk art have included an entire show of contemporary New Mexican lithographs and crafts and a display of historic Indian pottery.

The gallery is located in a historic building in a restoration area of downtown Forth Worth. The exhibition design employs Southwestern antiques, such as pharmacy cases and a 19th century buggy.

J. Dautriche, Louis XV-XVI commode, lacquer and gilt bronze.
Garrick C. Stephenson (New York).

Guignard, Louis XVI etagere—one of pair·(c. 1775), mahogany. Garrick C. Stephenson (New York).

Portrait of a Woman (19th century, America). Ricco-Johnson Gallery (New York).

Therien & Co.   811 Montgomery, San Francisco, CA 94113   (415) 781-6991   Monday-Friday: 9:30-5:30 or by appointment

Therien & Co., with its main galleries on three floors in historic Jackson Square, has recently opened an additional gallery in San Francisco's Union Square. Care is taken at both locations to exhibit a broad range of 17th and 18th-century furniture with appropriate period accessories, namely porcelains, mirrors, and decorations.

One can examine an early Ming lacquered cabinet in the octagon room of the Sutter Street gallery along with a stamped J.E. Fromageau secretaire-a-abat-tant and an early George II walnut chest on a stand from St. Giles House.

Perhaps the most comprehensive collection can be seen in the Jackson Square location. The spacious main floor gallery concentrates on unique and sometimes esoteric items of different origins while the second floor features oak and walnut country furniture. Rustic pieces are grouped in the lower gallery with a selection of fine antique flat weave carpets.

Thos. K. Woodard American Antiques and Quilts   835 Madison Ave., New York, NY 10021   (212) 988-2906   Monday-Saturday: 11-6

The gallery's specialization is antique American patchwork and applique quilts. From the early 19th century to the early 20th century, these works in excellent condition range from crib and children's bed sizes to double, queen, and king sizes. There are also early 19th-century hand-dyed and hand-woven blankets and coverlets. A selection of Amish quilts are used as wall art because they are extremely graphic and bold in color.

Not to be overlooked is the gallery's selection of early American country and painted furniture such as a Hepplewhite bracket base graduated four drawer blanket chest with original red paint and original brasses. Some other unusual furniture items include a sixty-inch diameter butcher table dating about 1780 with its original red paint and a corner cupboard in old blue paint. Enhancing the country American look are rag rugs, baskets, spoonware, hooked rugs, watercolors and gameboards.

The best
at the
Antique galleries

Fa Hua Jar, Ming Dynasty (16th century, China), 13" high, porcelain. Weisbrod & Dy (New York).

Mennonite log cabin pieced-quilt, *Barn Raising* (1865), 86" x 86", wool challis. America Hurrah Antiques (New York).

Bernard van Risenburgh, Louis XV commode. Atop: Massimiliano Soldani-Benzi bronzes flank Francesco Bertos bronze (all early 18th century). Rosenberg & Stiebel (New York).

Giles Grendy, walnut chair (c. 1740). Kentshire Galleries (New York).

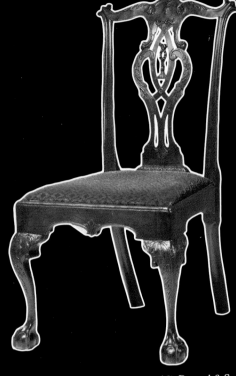

Philadelphia Chippendale chair (1 of 2). Bernard & S. Dean Levy. (New York).

George II Walnut Mirror. Malcolm Franklin (Chicago & New York).

The Goddess Kuan Yin, Ming
Dynasty (17th century China),
glazed stoneware. Ralph M. Chait
Galleries (New York).

Thomas Seymour, Satinwood
worktable. Berry Tracy (Goshen,
N.Y.).

Jade Mountain, K'ang Hsi period (1622-1722, China), 12″ high. Weisbrod & Dy (New York).

French sevres mounted atop vases (c. 1815). Earle D. Vandekar of
Knightsbridge (New York).

Blanket Chest (1789). Weathervane and Amish Quilt (1880).
Ricco-Johnson Gallery (New York).

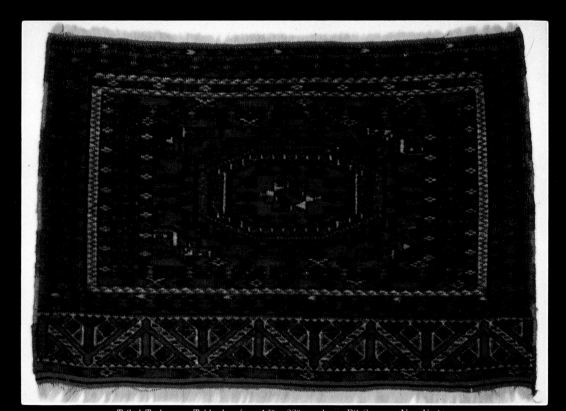

Tribal Turkoman Table-bag (mgn 1780 x 30"), rare, estr. FJ. Carpets (New York).

William & Mary bureau bookcase. Hyde Park Antiques (New York).

Queen Anne walnut bureau bookcase. Malcolm
Franklin (New York & Chicago).

John Aitken, cylinder desk & bookcase (1796-1800, Philadelphia).
Mahogany, satinwood, holly stringing. Berry Tracy (Goshen, N.Y.)

French provencial commode (18th century). Atop:
Louis XV candelabra, bronze. Michael Capo
Antiques (New York).

Oaxaca funerary urn (300-900 A.D.), 6" high, ceramic with
cinnabar. Bellas Artes (Santa Fe, N.M.)

George III serpentine commode. Hyde Park Antiques (New York).

Furniture &
Accessories
Galleries

Furniture &
Accessories
Galleries

By Location

California
Beverly Hills:
  Hansen
Encino:
  Redfern
Laguna Beach
  Yaekel
La Jolla:
  Ladner-Young
Palm Desert:
  Winfield Winsor
San Francisco:
  Dillingham, Domergue, Edwin,
  Shephard
Santa Monica:
  Gould
Colorado
Denver:
  Wilson
Connecticut
Jewett City:
  Walton
Woodbury:
  Dunton, Hammitt
Delaware
Wilmington:
  Stockwell
Florida
West Palm Beach:
  Surovek
Illinois
Chicago:
  Franklin, Varchmin
Winnetka:
  Fallen Oaks
Kentucky
Shelbyville:
  Wakefield-Scearce
Maryland
Bethesda:
  Secrest
Centreville:
  Young
Massachusetts
Boston:
  Billings
West Townsend:
  Delaney
Missouri
Clayton:
  Graves
St. Louis:
  Margo, Pass
New York
Goshen:
  Tracy
Millbrook:
  Stanton
New York City:
  Beshar, Blau, Capo, Didier Aaron,
  Franklin, Hyde Park, Kensington Pl.,
  Kentshire, Levy, Newel, Sack

North Carolina
Chapel Hill:
  Daniel, Whitehall
Greensboro:
  Faison
Raleigh:
  Danielson
Pennsylvania
Downington:
  Bradley
Fort Washington:
  Boyd
New Hope:
  Sandor
Philadelphia:
  Bullard, Finkel
Westchester:
  Schiffer
Yardley:
  Prickett

By Specializations

American:
  Boyd, Bradley, Capo, Daniel, Finkel,
  Didier Aaron, Dunton, Hammitt, Levy,
  Margo, Newel, Prickett, Sack, Sandor,
  Stallfort, Stanton, Stockwell, Tracy,
  Walton, Young
Chinese:
  Kensington Pl.
Clocks:
  Delany, Franklin, Levy, Prickett
English:
  Billings, Bullard, Capo, Danielson,
  Franklin, Gould, Graves, Didier Aaron,
  Dillingham, Edwin, Faison, Fallen Oaks,
  Franklin, Hansen, Hyde Park,
  Kensington Pl., Kentshire,
  Ladner-Young, Newel, Pass, Schiffer,
  Secrest, Shephard, Stanton, Varchmin,
  Wakefield-Scearce, Whitehall, Wilson,
  Winsor, Yaekel, Young
French:
  Capo, Domergue, Shephard, Yaekel
Rugs & Tapestries:
  Beshar, Vojtech Blau

A. Beshar & Company, Inc.   49 East 53rd St., 2nd fl., New York, NY 10022   **A. Beshar**
(212) 758-1400   Monday-Saturday: 9-5   June-August: closed Saturday

This firm has been in business since 1898 and is now in its third generation. A wide range of kinds and sizes of rugs are carried here. Over four thousand rugs fall into approximately four categories. The gallery handles new rugs to 20 years of age, semiantique rugs from 30-70 years of age, and antique rugs over 100 years old.

There is also a huge selection of classical rugs prior to 1775. These consist mainly of rugs from Persia, China, and Turkey. Among late 17th and early 18th-century rugs are Chinese Dragon carpets. There are also rare Turkish Ushak carpets. The inventory is constantly changing.

James Billings   70 Charles St., Boston, MA 02114   (617) 367-9533   **James Billings**
Monday-Saturday: 10-6

Located in the historic Charles Street meeting house at Mount Vernon Street, the new showrooms were opened in 1982 by James and Lise Billings as a branch of their businesses in London and Essex, England. The emphasis is on 18th-century English walnut, mahogany, and country furniture and Scandinavian painted furniture, with many interesting period decorative items.

The English furniture is mainly 18th-century and includes both sophisticated London-made salon and dining room furniture of walnut, mahogany, and satinwood with an occasional four-poster bed, bedside tables, and chests of drawers. Also handled are country pieces of oak, elm and the various fruitwoods, with emphasis on colour and good condition. The Scandinavian painted and decorated furniture includes tables, chairs, coffers, cupboards, and cradles of the 18th and early 19th centuries, many items being dated and most having the original paint.

A large selection of old Sheffield and silver-plated tableware is always available, together with period brass candlesticks, tea caddies, boxes and other decorative items. Period framed prints—mainly English— and English period portraits are also stocked.

Irvin & Delores Boyd/Meetinghouse Antiques   509 Bethlehem Pike, Fort   **Irvin & Delores**
Washington, PA 19034   (215) 646-5126   Daily: 9-5   **Boyd**

The shop is located in historic Fort Washington in the buildings of the Old Whitemarsh Friends Meetinghouse, adjacent to the Revolutionary War fort built during the Battle of Germantown. The business has been family owned for 25 years. The inventory consists mainly of 18th-century period furniture and country furniture prior to 1830. In the first and most important building, the 18th-century period furniture is housed. There is a fine selection of native hardwoods such as cherry, tigermaple, and walnut. Some of the pieces are signed and attributed to well known local cabinetmakers. Chests, slant front desks, corner cupboards, and clocks are some of the pieces offered. Fine examples of William and Mary, Queen Anne, and Chippendale styles exist here. The display of country furniture is in another building along with some semiformal period furniture. One can find a mixture of soft woods and hard woods in the form of corner cupboards, wall cupboards, desks, chairs, chests and blanket chests, tables, and some Oriental rugs. Throughout the shop are accessories that accent the furniture. There is a selection of lighting brass, pewters, mirrors, baskets, and rugs.

Philip H. Bradley

Philip H. Bradley Co.   East Lancaster Ave., Downington, PA 19335   (215) 269-0427   Monday-Saturday: 9-5

This gallery deals primarily in 18th-century American furniture and accessories with emphasis on pieces of Pennsylvania origin. Pieces range from the Queen Anne period in the early 18th century to 1830. There is always a selection of Pennsylvania highboys (high chests of four or five drawers) and lowboys (low chests designed like the lower section of a highboy, frequently with one long drawer over a row of three). Also available are spice cupboards in either walnut or cherry, found locally in Chester County and sometimes a rare spice cupboard will be on hand.

All kinds of 18th century accessories are handled and displayed throughout the shop. Chinese export porcelain made for the American market includes platters, cups, and saucers. American historical Staffordshire figures are shown as well as Pennsylvania slipware, china, and glass.

Mr. Bradley, who is always searching for rare items of the period, has carried a number of rare pieces from time to time, including a Joseph Richardson silver tankard, a pottery piece by William Lill or a scraffito ornament which was a Pennsylvania specialty.

Alfred Bullard, Inc.

Alfred Bullard, Inc.   1604 Pine St., Philadelphia PA 19103   (215) 735-1879   Monday-Friday: 10-4 or by appointment.

Founded in 1926 in Philadelphia, the gallery has been importing and specializing in fine English antiques ever since. Over the years, the concentration of the varied stock has come from the 18th century, although examples of the Jacobean and William and Mary periods are available. Also strongly emphasized are the decorative furnishings of Regency design. In the selection of antiques offered, special care is given to the quality of the woods and the patina (a green rust covering ancient metals) which cannot be replaced. The firm offers pieces that have not lost their 18th-century integrity.

Bullard's specializes in a wide range of looking glasses from the earlier, more architectural examples, through the elaborate Chippendale period to the neoclassic and Regency styles. Another strong department is dining room furniture, as there is always a large stock of sideboards, dining tables, and chairs.

The showrooms are organized as room settings to give the buyer the opportunity to see pieces in their domestic scale and arrangement. In addition to carrying a fine stock, the restoration and care of the pieces are of prime concern in the gallery.

Michael Capo   831 Broadway, New York, NY 10003   (212) 982-3356   *Michael Capo*
Monday-Saturday: 9:30-5

Located just east of Manhattan's Greenwich Village, the gallery offers a variety
of 17th-, 18th-, and 19th-century case pieces of furniture and accessories with
an eclectic mix of Early American, Louis XV, English Georgian, French
Provincial, and Italian Renaissance. One may find commodes by Giusseppi
Magiolini or an oversize marble-top French commode, sidechairs by George
Jacob, or an 18th-century Normandy marriage armoire. English bookcases and
Italian Portugese secretaries are also to be found.

   A smaller but unique selection of accessories are displayed on the walls and
in the vitrines. Of particular interest are the 19th-century genre paintings.
French and Russian chandeliers clutter the ceiling and from time to time one
may find Italian marble life-size statuary, Empire bronze-mounted clock sets,
and ivory tankards. There are also French silver candlesticks and bronze urns
on display.

Elizabeth R. Daniel   2 Gooseneck Rd., Chapel Hill, NC 27514   (919)   *Elizabeth R.*
968-3041   By appointment   *Daniel*

The gallery concentrates on American furniture of the 18th and early 19th
centuries. Fine furniture from many periods including Queen Anne, Sheraton,
Chippendale, and Hepplewhite are carried. Pieces run the gamut from large
highboys and drop-leaf tables and beds to smaller items such as mirrors and
candlestands. A variety of woods, such as maple, cherry, and mahogany are
shown. There are Windsor chairs by Connecticut furniture maker A. D. Allen
and New Yorker John Sproson.

   Though furniture predominates, some interesting accessories are found as
well. Early brass candlesticks, boxes, and brass andirons are represented
throughout the gallery. Eighteenth century English delftware such as plates,
bowls, and platters is also displayed. One may see a signed and labeled looking
glass by Paul Cermeneti of Boston or James Todd of Portland, Maine.

Arthur H. Danielson Antiques Ltd.   1101 Wake Forst Rd., Raleigh, NC   *Arthur H.*
27604   (919) 828-7739   Daily: 12-6   *Danielson*

Located near the heart of Raleigh and the Mordecai Historic Park with the
restored birthplace of President Andrew Johnson, this shop has provided
unique and interesting antique furniture and accessories for nearly 15 years.
Eclectic pieces are the specialty. English furniture and pottery of the 18th
century predominate although continental and early American furniture are
included as well.

   Always available are 18th-century English toby jogs (earthenware mugs
shaped as a seated figure, usually in the form of a stout man wearing a
three-cornered hat). There is also a good selection of Dutch delft and English
delftware (tin-glazed earthenware), creamware (cream-colored, lead-glazed
earthenware decorated in gold), salt-glazed ware (pottery glazed by throwing
salt into an oven during the firing process), and other earthenware objects.

   A wide range of furniture supplements the gallery's concentration on pieces
of 18th and early 19th-century England. Included are examples from the Italian
Renaissance, such as a walnut refectory table, as well as American items from
North Carolina, such as walnut corner cupboards. In addition, Oriental
porcelains from China and Japan are blended throughout the shop.

John and Barbara Delaney

John and Barbara Delaney   473 Main St., West Townsend, MA 01474   (617) 597-2231   Weekdays: by appointment, Saturday & Sunday: 9-5

This antique clock shop is located in a country village in north central Massachusetts, 50 miles northwest of Boston. The clocks are displayed in an 18th century colonial home, coachhouse, and barn. Emphasis is placed on the American tall clock, of which the Delaneys have a large selection. There are always examples of tall case clocks made by the Willard family. Also displayed are brass-dial long-case (grandfather) clocks by Nathaniel Muliken, Samuel Bagnell, and Isaac Brokaw. Many clocks from New Hampshire, Maine, Massachusetts, and Connecticut are always present along with examples from New Jersey, Pennsylvania, and New York. There are many wooden tall clocks by the Willard family, Seth Thomas, and Silas Hoadley. In addition, one can find Massachusetts shelf clocks by Aaron Willard and David Wood as well as a girandole, a type of ornamental banjo clock. There are several banjo, lyre, and mirror clocks here. The mirrors are those of New Hampshire, New York, and Connecticut. Although the collection is predominantly American, representations of English, Dutch, and French clocks are also on hand. Several pieces of early furniture are shown, such as highboys (American tall chests), Windsor chairs, and Regency barometers and orchronometers.

Didier Aaron

Didier Aaron, Inc.   32 East 67th St., New York, NY 10021   (212) 988-5248.   Monday-Friday: 10-6

An established French antiques firm in Paris, this townhouse gallery has been represented in New York for the past six years and in Los Angeles for almost two years. An eclectic collection resides in New York, comprising 18th-century furniture, art deco and oriental objects, English Biedermeier (1820-1850), American furniture, and a newly-installed old masters department.

Some of the 18th-century French furniture includes an Imperial Russian mahogany secretary ordered by Catherine II of Russia from David Roentgen, two pieces by Joseph Baumhauer, chairs made for Versailles by Jean Boucault, a suite of furniture by Phillippe Poirie, and furniture by J.H. Riesener and Canabas.

Oriental screens spanning three centuries mingle with Japanese bronze vases and a pair of 80-inch Japanese lanterns. Terra cotta sculpture by Carrier Belleuse is offset by furniture by Herter Brothers and Eastlake-style pieces (American Neo-Gothic furniture of the late 19th century). Nineteenth-century English Regency library steps flank a French Charles X pedestal table near a pair of Louis XVI candlesticks adorned with rams heads and a Russian 18th-century blue glass ormolu (golden bronze gilt) mounted vase. A 19th-century Indian chest is surrounded by Thai pottery.

The art deco furniture is amply represented by exceptional pieces by Emile-Jacques Ruhlmann, including a lit *soleil* in macassar veneer ebony on a frame of Hungarian oak and the desk of the *collectionneur* also by Ruhlmann, made for the Hotel du Collectionneur at the Arts Decoratifs exhibition of 1925. Other art deco items include works by Dunand and Lalique. The walls are filled with 19th-century paintings evoking the Belle Epoque and Victorian spirits. As one ascends to the third floor, old master paintings are visible.

Cabinet with cinnabar (19th century, Japan). Didier Aaron (New York).

Dillingham

Dillingham and Company   3485 Sacramento St., San Francisco, CA 94118
(415) 563-1976   Monday-Friday: 10-5

Founded in 1973, this gallery specializes in fine English and continental furniture and furnishings for the serious collector. In addition to furniture, some early English pottery, textiles, metalwork, and snuff boxes are always in stock. The period between 1670 and 1810 is emphasized.

Although most English furniture was not signed directly by the maker, stylistic variations sometimes make a solid attribution possible. On display is veneered walnut and oak furniture from the 17th and early 18th centuries as well as 18th-century mahogany and early 19th-century rosewood furniture. Dillingham will occasionally buy furniture and objects that are not English, but reflect the influence of English design. It is therefore usual to find some Portuguese and Dutch furniture displayed as well as occasional pieces of Indian furniture.

Setting off the furniture and broadening the scope of the gallery are fine tea caddies, 18th-century brass candlesticks, snuff boxes, and early primitive paintings. Often English or Irish nonacademic paintings are shown.

Robert Domergue

Robert Domergue & Company   560 Jackson St., San Francisco, CA 94133
(415) 781-4034   Monday-Friday: 9-5

Specialists in fine 18th-century French and Italian furniture, the gallery is located one block from San Francisco's landmark "pyramid" building in the Jackson Square Historic district. The gallery maintains a broad range of 18th-century furniture from France, Italy, and the continent. In French furniture, examples by the best Parisian makers contrast with work from the provinces. Pieces of marquetry (furniture on which thin pieces of wood are arranged and glued in a geometrical design) share the floor with provincial pieces in plain woods. There is always a fine selection of seat furniture. sometimes signed examples by eminent makers such as Georges Jacob, Cresson, and Le Large. In case furniture, among commodes of marquetry and parquetry (furniture inlay work in which pieces of different kinds and colors of woods were fitted to one another and applied in a geometric pattern), the finest provincial furniture is emphasized.

Mr. Domergue has a strong interest in French scenic wallpapers and displays work from factories such as those of Zuber and Dufour & Leroy. The Voyages of Captain Cook, Les Fetes Greques, and Paysages de Telemaque are or have been in stock.

Another focus of the gallery is Italian furniture. Painted furniture of the 18th

Haines & Holmes, card-table with trestle base (c. 1825, New York), mahogany. Berry Tracy (Goshen, N.Y.)

century is sought out and purchased whenever possible. The neoclassical period of the later 18th century is nearly always well represented. There are fruitwood commodes, painted and parcel gilt console tables, and interesting chairs showing the revival of Greek and Roman models.

Interspersed among the furniture are pieces of sculpture, a good collection of candlesticks, and pieces of faience (tin-glazed earthenware) and decorative paintings and drawings of the 18th century.

David Dunton

David Dunton Antiques   Rt. 132, Weekeepeemee Rd., Woodbury, CN 06798   (203) 263-5355   Daily: by appointment.

The gallery is located in the historic Hotchkissville section of Woodbury in the 1836 home of Gervaise Hotchkiss. The specialty here is American Federal furniture from 1790 to 1840. Emphasis is on formal furniture of the period rather than country. All types of pieces in mahogany, cherry, and maple are featured. Desks, dining room tables, chairs, sideboards, chests, and many other pieces are included in the styles of Hepplewhite, Sheraton, and the Empire period.

American paintings of the 19th and early 20th centuries, both academic and naive, are displayed throughout the gallery. One may see landscape, portrait, and genre paintings although they are not the main focus here. Accessories suitable to the American Federal period are handled as well. Exhibited are wallsconces and candlesticks in old Sheffield silver and firegilt, and decorative porcelain centerpieces from England and France.

Charles Edwin

Charles Edwin Antiques   3391 Sacramento St., San Francisco, CA 94118 (415) 346-8678   Tuesday-Saturday: 10-5

English furniture of the 18th century is offered in this modest showroom with emphasis on formal mahogany furniture and clocks from 1740 to 1800. The mahogany furniture dates back to 1675-1810, from William and Mary to George III styles. Included are Chippendale pieces, Hepplewhite, and the furniture of the Adam brothers with fluting, inlays, and classical motifs. There is dining room furniture, library furniture, bureaus, and chests. A few country pieces are to be found such as Welsh dressers, and oak and walnut bureaus and chests.

In addition to furniture, Georgian period clocks and 18th-century metalwork are offered. Long-case (grandfather) clocks and clocks by William Kipling (1720) are displayed. Always on hand are brass planters, jardinieres, and sundials. Snuffboxes, coffee pots, teapots, and tea urns are items to be seen as examples of japanned ware (Western imitation of Oriental lacquer works). A wide selection of Staffordshire figures is always offered.

Caroline Faison

Caroline Faison Antiques   18 Battleground Ct., Greensboro, NC 27408 (919) 272-0261   Monday-Friday: 10-4

The gallery has specialized for 18 years in 18th-century English furniture, which is purchased mainly in England several times per year. The shop consists of two houses moved together, in which each room is filled with English furniture and a few pieces of American furniture of the South. There are Oriental rugs on the floors, framed silk embroideries on the walls, and hundreds of English boxes and tea caddies scattered throughout the gallery. Also displayed are several Oriental and lacquer pieces, such as an 18th-century lacquer clock, a chinoiserie desk (decorated in a European version of Oriental motifs), and several lacquer boxes. There are several pieces of English oak, notably dresser bases and smaller furniture such as cricket and pub tables.

Complementing the furniture is a collection of porcelain. There are pieces from different English factories, including Worcester, Liverpool, and Caughley. Also displayed are delft porcelain (tin-glazed, blue-painted earthenware made in Holland from the mid-17th century), and Chinese export porcelain, such as blue and white and Canton.

Fallen Oaks

Fallen Oaks, Ltd.   1075 Gage St., Winnetka, Il 60093   (312) 446-3540
Tuesday-Saturday: 11-4:30 or by appointment

On display in this large suburban Chicago shop is an extensive collection of important early English oak furniture and related items from the 16th and 17th centuries. The gallery's representative English wooden pieces from medieval times once furnished either castles or cottages. Provenance is often available and many pieces have been exhibited or illustrated in furniture books. Pieces include a rare early 16th-century abbey table bearing the mark of Henry VIII, a coffer with the carved portrait of Edward VI, a bed dated 1621 from one of the most important stately homes in England, and a pair of cannons with armoral crests.

Every piece is described in detail, so you may browse freely. The owners are always glad to discuss the particulars of any piece with you. Variations in style relating to period or region of origin are visible in the works on display and close contact and comparison are encouraged. The shop's large library of early reference books, which is a center of oak research soon to be computerized, is available for consultation.

Contributing to the mood of the shop are accessories of the period including tapestries, brass and metalware, candlesticks and torchiers from 1450 to 1700, pictures, textiles, and wood and stone carvings, some dating from as early as 1300.

George I kneehole desk (c. 1725), burl walnut.
Malcolm Franklin (Chicago & New York).

M. Finkel & Daughter   936 Pine St., Philadelphia, PA 19107   (215) 627-7797   Monday-Friday: 10-5:30, Saturday: 11-5 except summer.

The gallery, located in the heart of Antiques Row, has been housed in an early 19th-century building adjacent to Society Hill for 35 years. Since 1975, the area of concentration has been Americana, both formal and country 18th and 19th-century furniture, antique quilts, and folk art.

There are two floors of American furniture, decorative arts, paintings, and textiles with strong emphasis on quilts and other textile folk art. The furniture always includes a strong selection of cupboards, tables, desks, tall case clocks, chests of drawers, and blanket chests as well as small items. Accessories include weathervanes, whirligigs, painted boxes, samplers, decoys, and early copper, brass, and iron objects.

The quilt display on the second floor is a panorama of color and texture, with upwards of a dozen large quilts displayed on the walls. Between 100 and 250 quilts are in stock, and they all date prior to 1940, with the majority being made in the late 19th century. Here, condition is paramount along with interesting design and fabrics. Amish, Mennonite, applique, and crib quilts are always on hand, and there is also an excellent selection of antique hook rugs and rag carpet runners.

Malcolm Franklin, Inc.   126 E. Delaware Place, Chicago, IL 60611   (312) 337-0202   (additional location at 15 E. 57th St., New York, NY 10022) Monday-Friday: 10-5:30

Located in both Chicago and New York, the gallery is based in Chicago's Water Tower area, just a few doors off North Michigan Avenue. Three generations of the Franklin family have offered fine English furniture dating from the beginning of wood veneering in the late 1600s to 1820. Though many periods and styles are represented, emphasis is on English walnut furniture. With founder Malcolm Franklin recently deceased, his son Paul and daughter Mary Ann Sullivan are now the sole owners.

The most important finds are located in the west room, at left as you enter the building. With few exceptions, the furniture is made of English walnut between 1680 and 1730. Though the gallery stresses that much of its furniture is not formally "labeled", many of the offerings are by great names among furniture makers of the period, including William Bell, Giles Grendy, William Old, John Ody, Elizabeth Bell, and Coxed and Worster. Pieces run the gamut from delicate chests and bureau-bookcases to tables and chairs. Long-case (grandfather) clocks by prominent London clockmakers are almost always on hand. It's not unusual to find perfectly-working time pieces by some of the most well-known 17th century makers, including Daniel Quare and Thomas Clowes.

The east room consists of fine furniture from many periods, encompassing the Chippendale, Hepplewhite, Sheraton, and Regency styles. Most of the diversified pieces are made from mahogany, rosewood, satinwood and yew wood. It is here that most of the accessories are displayed, including Staffordshire porcelain figurines and tableware. All the pieces in this room are from the mid-18th to the early 19th centuries.

The lower level consists of oak and country furniture, almost exclusively English, excepting occasional pieces from the continent. At times the room looks like an old English inn, complete with massive oak cupboards, Yorkshire dressers, and carved armchairs. Some pieces date as early as 1690, but most range from the early 18th century to 1820.

Edmund Card, longcase clock
(c. 1680, London), marquetry walnut &
ebony. Malcom Franklin (New York).

Caleb Wheaton, Hepplewhite longcase
clock (c. 1790, Providence, R.I.).
Bernard & S. Dean Levy (New York).

Though furniture predominates, interesting accessories are found in all three rooms. Staffordshire pottery is amply displayed in many of the bureaus along with tea caddies and brass candlesticks. Porcelain collections are at times extensive, dating from 1760 to 1860, including Worcester, Derby, and ironstone pieces. Barometers from 1760 to 1840 are almost always on hand. There are also good selections of English landscape and marine paintings, occasionally by prominent artists, though less emphasis is placed on wall pieces. Some embroideries and tapestries from around the world are also available.

Richard Gould

Richard Gould Antiques, Ltd.   216 26th, Santa Monica, CA 90402   (213) 395-0724   Monday-Friday: 10-4, Saturday: by appointment.

The gallery is a direct importer of period furniture and accessories of the 17th, 18th, and early 19th centuries, concentrating mainly on English and some American pieces. Predominating are English oak pieces, Welsh dressers, gate-leg tables (with twisted legs) and sideboards. Mahogany chests, dining room tables, lowboys (American flat-topped dressing tables with drawers), and desks are also featured. Many walnut pieces are on hand, including William & Mary cabinets, lowboys, and chests. English tall clocks are found here as well.

There are interesting accessories that can be found in the gallery, such as 18th and 19th-century brass candlesticks and hearth equipment, Georgian silver spoons, and Staffordshire porcelain. There are good selections of Chinese export porcelain, including famille rose, named after prominent rose pink. Pieces such as plates, punchbowls, and some enamels predominate. There are early 19th-century Chinese export silver teakettles on stands and an assortment of christening mugs. Though the gallery does not emphasize wall hangings, there are good selections of Chinese export watercolors and paintings of Chinese ladies, ships, flowers, and mandarin figures.

Clark Graves

Clark Graves Antiques   132 N. Meramec, Clayton, MO 63105   (314) 715-2695   Tuesday-Saturday: 9:30-5

Located in a suburb of St. Louis, the gallery is in one of the city's oldest farmhouses, which was built around 1870. The shop consists of four showrooms and specializes in 18th- and 19th-century furniture, porcelains, and accessories that accompany 18th- and 19th-century interiors. The shop is usually filled with English 18th- and 19th-century oak, walnut, and mahogany furniture. Most of the pieces are purchased in the United Kingdom and represent all periods from Queen Anne to Regency. Some of the items usually seen are secretaries, Hepplewhite chests, and Sheraton sideboards. Occasionally there are a few pieces of American Federal furniture.

Another feature of the gallery is 18th-century English and continental porcelains of Worcester, Derby, and Rockingham as well as Chinese export porcelain. A unique feature of the gallery is English garden furniture including lead garden figures, animals, and wire and iron benches and chairs.

Kenneth Hammitt

Kenneth Hammitt Antiques, Inc.   Main St. South, Woodbury, CN 06789 (203) 263-5676   Monday-Saturday: 10-5:30

The gallery, conveniently located for over 25 years on Route 6 in one of Woodbury's historic districts, is housed in a colonial home included on the National Register of Historic Places. The building, which dates from the 1750s includes 10 rooms of period antiques and accessories.

American period furniture dominates the inventory from Queen Anne (early 18th century) and Chippendale (1760-1776) through the Federal Period (1785-1830). This includes noteworthy case pieces as well as tables, chairs, and stands. It is the intention of the shop to provide examples of period furniture with a written guarantee as to authenticity.

Complementing the furniture collection are appropriate accessories including mirrors, fireplace equipment, lighting devices, and smaller decorative objects. Usually on hand is an extensive English delftware selection, early Sheffield silver-plate serving pieces, and a variety of paintings and Oriental rugs.

James M. Hansen

James M. Hansen   27 East De La Guerra, Santa Barbara, CA 93101   (805) 963-6827   Monday-Friday: 10-5

The specialty of the gallery is 18th-century English furniture and late-19th and early-20th-century American paintings. The furniture represents the Queen Anne style, characterized by elegant, curved forms, and the Chippendale style, associated with Thomas Chippendale, whose designs embraced a variety of styles such as Rococo, Chinese, Queen Anne, and Gothic. Items on display are barometers, bookcases, breakfronts, George II (1727-60) sidechairs, and Bombay cabinets (delicately-carved furniture in Indian style noted for elaborate geometric patterns inlaid in ebony and ivory).

There is also a display of 18th-century miniature furniture, including chests and beds. Chinese export porcelain, mostly 19th century, is scattered throughout the gallery. Always available is a selection of basins, pitchers, tureens, and dishes. English tea caddies are carried as well.

The paintings consist of works by many early California artists, such as Charles Partridge Adams (landscapes), Alexander Harmer (landscapes of California and Mexico and Indians), Colin Campbell Cooper (American and European landscapes), Ralph Holmes (Western landscapes, notably Yosemite and Grand Canyon), John Gamble (California wildflowers), and Gordon Coutts (figures and landscapes).

Also handled at the gallery are Audubon originals, including pelicans, eider ducks, and several quadrupeds.

Hyde Park

Hyde Park Antiques, Ltd.   836 Broadway, New York, NY 10003   (212) 477-0033   Monday-Friday: 9-5:30; Saturday: 10-3 except June-Labor Day

At the heart of New York's fastest growing center for fine antiques, Hyde Park is housed in a spacious and elegant historic castiron building. The two large, carpeted gallery floors with architectural columns topped with Corinthian capitals, contain an extensive collection of 17th-, 18th-, and early 19th-century English furniture. A broad interest is demonstrated by the scope of the collection, which usually features at least two dozen 18th-century sideboards and at least half that many Georgian breakfront bookcases at any one time, as well as pieces of the Queen Anne, Charles II, and William and Mary periods.

Fine ceramics and sporting art are two other specialties of wide selection in the gallery. Chinese export punchbowls painted with scenes of Mandarin court life or British hunts jostle with such rarities as a pair of large-scale, first-period, Worcester pavillion-pattern covered tureens and stands. In the center of the showroom is a four-pedestal Sheraton dining table, on which rests an ironstone dinner service for fourteen, complete with sauce ladles. Across the room is a satinwood neoclassical commode attributed to Thomas Chippendale.

Kensington Place Antiques   80 E. 11th St., New York, NY 10003   (212) 533-7652   Monday-Friday: 10-5

Kensington Place

The main emphasis of this gallery is on English and continental decorative furniture and objects. Several pieces of English Regency furniture of the early 19th century are represented. On hand are a pair of cabinets painted in simulated zebra wood with brass cornices in the style of Thomas Hope. Among the Russian furniture is a console table of 1810 with guilt griffins as support and an architectural mirror.

A selection of Chinese furniture is offered as well. There is a colorful Chinese screen of 1800 with pink and green colors on a dark brown background. Also colorful are a pair of Chinese red cinnabar lacquer cabinets with doors and drawers. There are good selections of English and French painted tole (painted tinware) and papier-mache.

In addition to 18th- and 19th-century English botanical prints, the gallery maintains a large stock of framed decorative prints. Among these are works by 17th-century Dutch artist Basilus Besler, 18th-century English artist Edwards, and 19th-century English artist Paxton.

Kentshire Galleries, Ltd.   37 East 12th St., New York, NY 10003   (212) 673-6644   Monday-Friday: 9-5; Saturday: 9-1, except June, July, August

Kentshire

The firm occupies an entire eight-story building with a beautiful cast iron front, vaulted ceilings, and architectural columns. Kentshire displays its tremendous inventory on seven of its eight floors. The eighth floor houses an excellent restoration shop.

The main focus is on English furniture of the 18th and 19th centuries. All of the important periods are well represented, including Charles II, William and Mary, Queen Anne, George II and III, Regency, and William IV.

Typical examples are an important 18th-century fiddleback mahogany breakfront, a pair of gilded Sheraton period armchairs, a rare George II four partner's desk, a Charles II japanned cabinet on its original silver gilt stand, and a George II naval admiral's desk. Also displayed are a William and Mary oyster walnut-veneered chest, a George I reverse painted Chinese scene in a carved gilt frame, an eleven-foot-long architectural pine bookcase, a set of eight painted Regency dining chairs, and a George III amboyna bookcase.

Other furniture in the collection includes sets of dining chairs in Queen Anne, Chippendale, and Regency styles, single and pairs of armchairs, unusual occasional chairs such as a French brass armchair with a leather seat, Sheraton and Hepplewhite sideboards, Georgian breakfronts, and console tables, lowboys, and chests.

Many accessories adorn the furniture, such as pairs of oriental vases, English porcelain, inkstands, tea caddies, silver-plated candlebras, brass candlesticks, ironstone tureens and platters, and garniture sets. Hanging on the walls is an extensive collection of paintings ranging from hunt scenes to Regency floral still lifes, landscapes, and seascapes. Numerous mirrors vary from Georgian gilt, mahogany, and walnut mirrors, to carved pine mirrors, Venetian, Irish, and French mirrors.

The gallery also has a very large selection of country furniture, such as pine servers, cabinets, bookcases, and dressers, and oak lowboys and dressers, as well as sets of chairs, armoires, and farm tables, in addition to the accessories that go with them. The inventory from England and the United States changes quickly at Kentshire.

175

Ladner-Young

Ladner-Young, Inc.   414 La Canada, La Jolla, CA 92037   (619) 459-3753
Monday-Friday: 8:30-5

Located on a quiet street one block east of La Jolla Blvd., the shop is a colonial cottage where four rooms of furniture are shown. A full, representative line of dressy English country furniture from the 17th, 18th, and 19th centuries is featured. Included are Queen Anne pieces produced until 1760 and pieces of all types dating up to 1830. Always in stock are formal bureaus and Welsh dressers (side tables with drawers and shelves in the cottage style).

The furniture, which includes many types of wood, notably mahogany and walnut, is purchased in England. Complementing the furniture are English prints, among the few decorative items on display.

Bernard & S. Dean Levy

Bernard & S. Dean Levy Inc.   981 Madison Avenue, New York, NY 10021
(212) 628-7088   Tuesday-Saturday: 9:30-5:30   June-September:
Monday-Friday: 9:30-5:30

An extensive selection of American antiques is shown throughout this large, second-floor gallery, including pieces from the late 17th, 18th, and early 19th centuries. Emphasis is placed on examples made in New England, New York, Pennsylvania, and the southern states during these periods. Pieces made by the great cabinetmakers such as the Townsends and the Goddards, Jonathan Gostelowe, Thomas Tufft, Michael Allison, Slover and Taylor, and Duncan Phyfe are represented either by careful attribution or authenticating labels.

The entire range of American furniture arts is found here. On display are Queen Anne and Chippendale highboys and lowboys, blocked-front and serpentined chests, slant-front desks and secretaries including rare bombe examples, and stately Federal period sideboards, card tables, and dining tables. Also shown are chair forms from all periods, small work tables, tea tables, poster beds, and numerous looking glasses in a variety of designs. With the intent of having the full spectrum of America's decorative heritage available, provincial furniture arts have been included in the gallery's rooms. Examples are painted pieces such as decorated blanket chests, and a wide presentation of Windsor seating pieces.

Another major additon to the gallery has been the Katharine Prentis Murphy Collection, formerly exhibited at the New York Historical Society, known for its rare Jacobean, William and Mary, and early Queen Anne furniture of New England origin, as well as the earliest American portraits. Included in the collection are several rare pieces including a highboy once owned by the famous Revere family. Long-case (grandfather) clocks by foremost makers such as Aaron Willard, Caleb Wheaton, Wood & Hudson, and Isaac Doolittle, are displayed together with shelf clocks.

Appropriate accessories which decorated homes during the Colonial and Federal periods are found on shelves in the gallery. They hold American silver wares, Chinese export porcelain, delft pottery, early brass candlesticks, pewter pieces, and a group of redware pottery from the Lorimer Collection.

American paintings are on view in a section of the gallery. The concentration is on American 19th and early 20th-century artists, with works by William Harnett, Albert Bierstadt, J. G. Brown, Thomas Hovenden, George Henry Hall, Theodore Robinson, Martin Johnson Heade, Henry Inman, Eastman Johnson, Reginald Marsh, John Frederick Kensett, and John Marin, among others.

Chippendale pole-screen (c. 1780, Salem, MA.), Bernard & S. Dean Levy (New York).

William & Mary highboy (c. 1700, Boston), walnut, maple & pine. Bernard & S. Dean Levy (New York).

Margo　　Margo Antiques　　4660 Maryland Ave., St. Louis, MO 63108　　(314) 367-1177　　Monday-Saturday: 11-4

The shop has been located in the Central West End district of Saint Louis for over 50 years and deals mainly in American formal and country furniture until 1825. Examples throughout the shop consist of Windsor chairs, Hitchcock chairs, Hepplewhite chests and Chippendale mirrors. Scattered about are period accessories such as Queen Anne candlestands dating about 1870.

There is always a large selection of pottery, including English delft, Wieldon plates and teapots, Wedgewood, and older examples of soft pottery such as Pre-Columbian, Mexican, Peruvian, Costa Rican, and excavated American Indian pieces. The porcelains include Bow, Worcester and other hard paste porcelains. One will find an assortment of Staffordshire figures as well. In addition, there is early American blown and pressed glass, Schrimshaw whales teeth, walrus tusks, Luristan bronze, African gold weights and artifacts, powder horns, early prints, and silhouettes.

Newel　　Newel Art Galleries, Inc.　　425 East 53rd St., New York, NY 10022　　(212) 758-1970　　Monday-Friday: 9-5

The galleries are located in a six-story building housing 45,000 square feet of furniture and accessories from the Renaissance to the art deco period. The first floor concentrates on accessories which include red Chinese dogs, enormous dragons, and numerous crystal chandeliers hanging from the ceiling. The second floor holds carved teakwood Burmese furniture, Spanish furniture, and complete paneled rooms in English Tudor, Gothic, and Jacobean styles. The third floor contains art deco and art nouveau pieces, Victorian furniture, and some paintings. The fourth floor offers examples of English and American lacquer pieces, and Chippendale, Sheraton, and English Regency furniture. The fifth floor houses a collection of 18th- and 19th-century French and Italian continental pieces. Even in the basement is an 1882 Brunswick pool table, wicker and iron objects, hat racks, and easels. Throughout the entire collection, one can see traditional settings, but the eye focuses mainly on the unusual here—the off-beat which adds a unique twist to this gallery and its extensive inventory.

Jules L. Pass　　Jules L. Pass Antiques, Ltd.　　9916 Clayton Rd., St. Louis, MO 63124　　(314) 991-1522　　Monday-Saturday: 10-5

Mr. Pass, a long-time collector of antiques, recently moved his gallery to this larger location in a suburb of St. Louis to better incorporate the furniture into several room settings. The gallery specializes in 18th- and early 19th-century English furniture, for which the owner makes several trips to England yearly. Always available are examples of early 18th-century walnut bureau bookcases (fall-front desks with a bookcase top). Walnut chests and lowboys are featured as well. Special emphasis is placed on mahogany pieces through the 1820s including chests and desks. Prime examples of English oak furniture concentrating on Welsh dressers are displayed with Staffordshire figurines. Eighteenth century Chinese export porcelain, including teapots, plates, and soup tureens, as well as 18th- and 19th-century English porcelain are placed throughout the shop. A large collection of period English tea caddies ranging from ivory to mahogany is also exhibited. Oil paintings are mostly early 19th-century English naive, primitive or animal paintings.

C. L. Prickett, Inc.   930 Stoney Hill Rd., Yardley, PA 19067   (215) 493-4284   Monday-Saturday: 10-5

Located in Lower Bucks County, 35 minutes northeast of Philadelphia, this gallery sits on five acres of farmland and is housed in an 18th-century barn. There are 10 rooms of settings here concentrating on Americana. There is both formal and country furniture although the gallery places more emphasis on the formal pieces. All periods from Queen Anne to Hepplewhite are included. On the first floor one will find Pennsylvania desks and chests, as well as Connecticut pieces, which are lighter in form compared to those from Pennsylvania, such as highboys, lowboys and desks. An important part of the gallery is the collection of tall case clocks. There is always a selection of 1780 Pennsylvania tall case clocks characterized by the broken arch tops, Roxbury case clocks by Simon Willard of Massachusetts, and from time to time a Joakin Hill clock from Flemington, New Jersey, and clocks by David Woods from Newberry Port, Massachusetts.

The second floor houses the country and less formal pieces of American furniture. Selections of Windsor chairs, hutch tables, and trestle tables are found here as well as country beds. Throughout the gallery are 19th-century American paintings. One can see work by Philadelphia artists Thomas Hope and Robert Street displayed. Many unsigned landscapes and portraits of the period are on hand. Though not the rule, the gallery has handled the work of Grandma Moses and her son, Forest Moses, who paints landscapes as well.

English Regency secretaire/breakfront bookcase (c. 1810), rosewood with brass inlay. Hyde Park Antiques (New York).

Israel Sack

Israel Sack, Inc.   15 East 57th St., New York, NY 10022   (212) 753-6562
Monday-Friday 9:30-5:00; Saturday: 10:30-3:30   July-August: Closed Saturday

Regarded by many as the premier dealer in American furniture, the establishment takes up two floors. Now operated by sons of founder Israel Sack—Albert, Harold and Robert— the emphasis has not changed. The tradition of regarding American craftsmen as among the finest in the world has won Sack the opportunity to furnish some of America's most important collections including Williamsburg, and many Museums.

To the uninitiated eye, the floors are crowded with what appears to be English furniture. The Sacks are quick to point out that most of the better American pieces are much more vertical than their English counterparts and less ornate. American makers were more concerned with form, line and unity. They also point out that in England simple furniture was made by lesser craftsmen, but in America simple furniture was made by top craftsmen.

Sack is one of the few places to find furniture from the Pilgrim period. Most of it was made in the 17th century with the general school of design of England. Though the Sacks regard such pieces as an art form, many are more primitive than most of the galleries offering. Most furniture of this period is made from oak and pine, somewhat resembling English country furniture of the same period. Makers of this period are rarely identifiable and are therefore attributed to areas, most commonly Boston, Salem and Newport.

Sack also has a good selection of William and Mary pieces. Almost all of the finer offerings are made of walnut. It is not uncommon to find some pieces of the great names in American furniture making such as Benjamin Randolph and Goddard-Townscend.

Queen Anne styles of American furniture from the period 1720 to 1730 are almost always in abundance. Most of these pieces can be divided into two categories—those made in rural areas and those made by urban makers. The better pieces come from Boston makers such as William Savory, Duncan Phyfe and John Seymour. The woods are walnut veneer, solid Pennsylvania walnut and mahogany. Most of the rural furniture is made from native woods such as cherry and maple.

H. and R. Sandor

H. and R. Sandor, Inc.   Route 202, P. O. Box 207, New Hope, PA 18938   (215) 862-9181   Monday-Saturday: 10-4

In 1973, the Sandors located their business in an early 18th century fieldstone house, Ingham Manor, in Bucks County, Pennsylvania. Ingham Manor retains a raised paneled interior and an early kitchen wing, which makes an effective background for their formal as well as less formal and country pieces. Collecting and selling American antique furniture is the mainstay of the gallery. Most pieces are formal 18th-century American furniture made during the Queen Anne, Chippendale, and Federal periods. On hand from these periods are chairs, chests, desks, and dining room tables. Also available are highboys (tall chests of drawers) and sideboards (dining room pieces used for holding table ware).

In addition to furniture, there is also a good selection of 18th- and 19th-century American paintings by such notables as landscape painters Edward Willis Redfield and the Smith Brothers, and portraits by Ami Phillips and Thomas Sully. Paintings by 19th-century artist Severin Roesen are important additions to the gallery.

Among the pieces of furniture, decorative period accessories are displayed. Eighteenth-century brass candlesticks and ink stands are placed throughout

Walnut secretaire (c. 1800), Hyde Park Antiques (New York).

the rooms. Delftware, which is tin-glazed earthenware from England or the Low countries, and Chinese exportware are also exhibited.

Herbert Schiffer

Herbert Schiffer   1469 Morstein Rd., West Chester, PA 19380   (215) 696-1001   Monday-Friday: 9-5, Saturday: 9-4

Located in a barn with about 6000 square feet of space, this gallery has had much to show in its 30 years in business. One of its specialties is English city and country furniture from the late 17th century to the early 19th century. There are about 15 rooms of furniture to be seen. Many different types of wood are available, such as mahogany, walnut veneer, walnut, cherry, poplar, and pine. Items vary from banquet tables to sets of chairs and blanket chests.

Pennsylvania walnut furniture is the primary interest here, however, English oak joint stools and Sheraton card tables are on hand. Another specialty of the gallery is mirrors. There are always about 50 mirrors in stock from the Queen Anne, Chippendale, and Sheraton periods.

The gallery also handles a great deal of Canton, rose medallion, and English pottery. Also on display are English delft, Pennsylvania redware (a simple type of American domestic pottery) and slipware (earthenware decorated with a diluted clay mixture) as well as Leeds creamware (cream-colored earthenware).

Mark Secrest

Mark Secrest Inc.   4920 Hamden Lane, Bethesda, MD 20814   (301) 654-4320   Monday-Friday: 9-5, Saturday: 10-3 or by appointment

The gallery features English furniture from 1670 to 1800, particularly mahogany pieces from 1730 to 1750. Items of this period on display include case furniture (pieces such as a chest or cupboard used for storage), sideboards (pieces of dining furniture used for holding tableware), tallboys (tall chests of drawers), library chairs (chairs with steps under the seat for turning over into a step unit), and occasional tables.

Though furniture predominates, 19th-century European paintings are shown as well. Nineteenth-century landscape painters of the English school are represented by Sidney Richard Percy, Edward Charles Williams, and Edwin Boddington.

A studio for restoration of furniture and conservation of paintings is also located in the gallery.

Norman Shephard

Norman Shephard   458 Jackson St., San Francisco, CA 94111   (415) 362-4145   Monday-Friday: 9-5

Both showrooms of the gallery feature 17th-, 18th-, and 19th-century English and French furniture with stress on the unusual. Chests, dining room tables, and sets of chairs can always be found in all types of wood. Special emphasis is given to overscaled cabinets, armoires, and sideboards of the period. In 37 years, Mr. Shepherd has stressed the unusual, carrying such items as the side of an 18th-century English carriage, circular 18th century library steps, and a carved pine eagle.

Shown throughout the gallery are Chinese porcelains of the 17th, 18th, and 19th centuries. All types of items can be found, such as teapots, cups and saucers, platters, and tureens.

Stallfort

Stallfort Antiques   R. R. #1, Box 173, Elverson, CA 19520   (215) 286-5882   Tuesday-Saturday: 10-5

The main specialty here is American furniture of the William and Mary period,

Jonathon Gostelowe, Chippendale chest (c. 1760, Philadelphia), mahogany & white cedar. Bernard & S. Dean Levy (New York).

recognized by its ball feet, and Queen Anne style furniture produced as late as 1760. Stallfort features these two distinct styles with emphasis on country forms. The antiques are exhibited in two period houses and the rooms are furnished functionally and in keeping with period and decorative motifs of Colonial America. Both Pennsylvania and New England styles are represented in walnut, cherry, maple, and soft woods such as tulip, poplar, and pine. Some important finds are tavern tables, ladderback chairs (both arm and side), and Windsor chairs including one by Ebenezer Tracy, a late 18th-century Connecticut chairmaker. Cupboards, both hanging and standing, as well as chests and desks are generally found.

The gallery also exhibits 18th-century naive paintings as well as Oriental rugs from Persia, Afghanistan, and Iraq. There is also American pewter signed by such important makers as Ashbil Griswold of Connecticut, George Lightner of Maryland, and Parks Boyd of Pennsylvania.

Joyce Harris Stanton

Joyce Harris Stanton, Antiques and Interiors   Franklin Ave., Millbrook, NY 12545   (914) 677-5511   Monday-Saturday: 11-4, Sunday: 1-5

This gallery is located in Dutchess County just 85 miles north of New York City. Mrs. Stanton offers fine 19th-century English and American furniture as well as decorations of the 18th and early 19th centuries. Presented in individual vignettes, there is furniture of many periods including Chippendale, Hepplewhite, Sheraton, Regency, Colonial, and Federal. There is a fine selection of early Engish Chippendale mirrors and mahogany sideboards (a piece of dining room furniture used for holding tableware). A Constantine game table and a 19th century mahogany drop leaf table are also on hand. Pieces of various woods in walnut, mahogany, satinwood, oak, yew wood, cherry and pine are displayed as well.

Not to be overlooked are primitive landscapes, portraits, and paintings by 19th-century American artists such as Edward Gaye and H.W. Kemper. Nineteenth century English animal paintings by Thomas Blinks are also displayed. Mrs. Stanton also carries single prints and sets of prints of different periods as well as botanical and hunting prints and watercolors.

Fine period accessories and handsome porcelain, brass or Chinese export lamps complete each vignette. There is usually a selection of Worcester, Derby, Newhall, and Chinese export porcelain.

David Stockwell

David Stockwell, Inc.   3710 Kennett Pike, P. O. Box 3840, Wilmington, DE 19807   (302) 655-4466   Monday-Friday: 9:30-5

Founder David Stockwell has been a collector in the antique business over 45 years. He started as an apprentice in the shop of Francis Brintonand and succeeded with his own shops in West Chester and Philadelphia, Pennsylvania, before moving to Delaware in 1956. The specialization of the gallery is American furniture of the 18th and early 19th centuries.

There are 20 rooms of period American furniture with concentrations in the Queen Anne and Chippendale periods with emphasis on Philadelphian examples. Among the pieces are many exceptional Baltimore sideboards, furniture named after the city in which it was produced. Card tables and Pembroke tables (occasional tables with a drop leaf on each side), can be seen as well. In addition to the Federal period (1785-1830), the Empire period (1810-40), characterized by bulky and showy furniture of Napoleonic influence, is also represented. On hand are tall case clocks, especially those from Philadelphia and Newport.

Duncan Phyfe, school-back side chair (c. 1820, New York),
mahogany, ash & tulip poplar. Berry Tracy (Goshen, N.Y.).

On the lower level are early pieces, trestle and tavern tables, ladder back and Windsor chairs, and a William and Mary chest. Displayed along with the furniture are pieces of redware and slipware pottery as well as Chinese export porcelains and English fireplace accessories.

Berry Tracy

Berry Tracy, Inc.   223 Main St., Goshen, NY 10924   (914) 294-7716
By appointment

Located just 50 minutes from the George Washington Bridge, this furniture exhibition gallery is on the ground floor of the Old Masonic temple, which was the old Federal Building restored in 1924, and across from the Museum of the Hall of Fame of the Trotter, which honors the invention of harness racing in Goshen.

Exhibited are 35-40 pieces of mostly Federal Period (1786-1826) mahogany and satinwood furniture by such famous American cabinetmakers as Duncan Phyfe, Charles Honore Lannuier, Michael Allison of New York, John and Thomas Seymour of Boston, Connoloy, and Adam Hains and Joseph Barry of Philadelphia. Most styles carried here are classical and range from the late 18th century inlaid Hepplewhite style and the Sheraton style (1790-1805), to early 19th century Regency period of Phyfe and the later Greek revival of 1830.

Mr. Tracy, a past curator of Decorative Arts in the American Wing of The Metropolitan Museum of Art in New York City, is a great lover and collector of clocks. Thus, a selection of clocks is displayed throughout the gallery. There are mostly clocks of the Federal Period, including tall clocks by Taber, John Brokaw, and Simon Willard.

James Varchmin

James Varchmin   620 North Michigan Ave., Ste. 310, Chicago, IL 60611
(312) 642-4266   Monday-Saturday: 10-6

Quality pieces in pristine condition are emphasized. The inventory begins historically with furnishings crafted during the reign of William and Mary (1689-94) and culminates with the English Soverign William IV (1830-37). Queen Anne, Chippendale, Hepplewhite, Sheraton, and Regency are familiar periods in this showroom. Warm woods with good colour appear in elm, mahogany, rosewood, satinwood, yew wood, and walnut. Always in stock is an array of chests, chairs, breakfront bookcases, lowboys (short-legged chests), long-case or grandfather clocks, and mirrors. In addition to furniture, accessory items are offered. Staffordshire porcelains are frequently represented as well as 18th- and 19th-century oil paintings. Tapestries, such as 16th- and 17th-century Flemish verdure tapestries known for their leafy landscapes, are occasionally featured.

Vojtech Blau

Vojtech Blau Inc.   800 B Fifth Ave., New York, NY 10021   (212) 249-4525   Monday-Friday: 8:30-4:30

Rare Persian, Turkish, Chinese, Caucasian, and European rugs dating from the 16th to 19th centuries are the specialties of the gallery. They range in size from small prayer rugs to room and palace sizes. Some of the rugs in Mr. Blau's collection include an early 19th-century Serapi Persian carpet, a Sileh rug from the region of the Caucasus, an 18th-century Bergano rug from Asia Minor, a 19th-century Bakhshayesh garden carpet from Northwest Persia, and a Zejwa rug from the Kouba District dating about 1800. There are also tapestries from Europe as early as the 16th century.

Mr. Blau arrived in New York in 1961. He had been a rug dealer in

Chippendale card-table (c. 1755, New York), mahogany. Bernard & S. Dean Levy, (New York).

Czechoslovakia before establishing himself here. He attempts to educate his customers about the rugs. A workshop on the premises handles the restoration and maintenance.

Wakefield-Scearce

Wakefield-Scearce Galleries, Inc.   525 Washington St., Shelbyville, KY 40065   (502) 633-4382   Monday-Saturday: 9-5

The galleries are located mid-way between Louisville and Lexington in historic Science Hill, once a prominent girl's school for 150 years. The building, which dates back to the 1790s, now houses unique specialty shops including this gallery, which specializes in 18th- and 19th-century English furniture and silver. The authentic room settings display the furniture and accessories to the best advantage. One may see a mahogany secretary breakfront bookcase, a bow-side serving table, a walnut Queen Anne highboy, and a George II Queen Anne style secretary. These are just a few of the many unusual pieces to be seen.

Displayed along with the furniture are accessories of the period. Paintings by J. F. Herring and Charles Towne and portraits by Allan Ramsay (1750) are on hand. English porcelain is exhibited on the dining tables, breakfronts, and occasional tables as well. Collections of Worcester dessert services and limited edition porcelains by the late Dorothy Doughty, which are models of birds and flowers, as well as other porcelain figures are exhibited.

The silver is housed in a separate building although some is displayed along with the furniture. The gallery emphasizes the work of Matthew Boulton. One can always see 50-60 Boulton items ranging from cruet sets and other small items to candlesticks, candelabras, and large tureens. Not to be overlooked are silver items by Paul Storr, the Bateman family, including the work of Hester Bateman, and Frenchman Paul de Lamerie.

John Walton

John Walton, Inc.   Box 307, Jewett City, CT 06351   (203) 376-0862 Open daily by appointment.

Located in southeastern Connecticut near Norwich, the gallery is housed in three early 18th-century buildings. Most of the inventory which concentrates in 17th-, 18th-, and early 19th-century American furniture is located in the barn. Both country and formal pieces are included here. The inventory, one of the largest in New England, boasts examples of William and Mary, Queen Anne, Chippendale, Hepplewhite, and Sheraton period pieces. The stock is constantly changing, however one can usually find chairs, chests, highboys, corner cabinets, and bookcases in assorted woods. From time to time, some documented pieces signed by important cabinetmakers will be on hand. Some of the pieces are displayed in the second building, a house not far from the large barn, and in a third, smaller early 17th-century house on the site.

John S. Walton, the founder of the gallery, has had 52 years experience in antiques.

Whitehall Shop

The Whitehall Shop   1215 E. Franklin St., Chapel Hill, NC 27514   (919) 942-3179   Monday-Saturday: 10-5, Sunday: 1-5

The gallery has offered English furniture and European accessories for over 51 years. Though many periods and styles are represented, emphasis is on 18th-century furnishing and objects. The most formal pieces are arranged in the front and middle rooms, featuring a selection of bureau bookcases, secretaries, sideboards, and occasional tables. Long-case grandfather clocks and breakfronts are often displayed in the side rooms along with dining tables and chairs. There is a wide selection of English silver as well. Coffee and tea services, entree dishes, revolving tureens, miniatures, and trays are offered. The Georgian silver collection includes Hester Bateman pieces and antique Sheffield, which is copper-plated with silver.

The lower level consists of oak and country furniture almost exclusively English. Some pieces date from the William and Mary period, but most range from the 18th to the mid-19th centuries. Though furniture predominates, there is a good collection of early English porcelain including Worcester and Derby, and a wide range of Oriental porcelains, carvings, and lacquerwares.

Wilson Galleries   1609 17th St., Denver, CO 80202   (303) 297-9103
Tuesday-Saturday: 10-5

Wilson

Founded in London in 1929, the gallery is now in its fourth American location in historic downtown Denver. Located directly across from the landmark Oxford Hotel, the gallery offers selections of fine period English furniture. While no specific emphasis is placed on any one period, a selection ranging in date from Charles II to Regency (early 19th century) can always be found. Such noted makers as Grinling Gibbons, Coxed and Worster, Philip and Elizabeth Bell, and Thomas Bullock have crossed the threshold. Also displayed are numerous items reflecting the influence of Chippendale, Hepplewhite, and Sheraton styles of furniture from delicate children's chairs to large cabinets. A diversified selection of woods is used, not only in construction, but also in decorative veneers (thin layers of overlaying wood applied to an inferior, less decorative wood). Mulberry, West Indian sabicu, Brazilian kingwood, rosewood, and tulipwood can often be found incorporated in the furniture. Occasionally a good selection of tea caddies, boxes, and needleworks is on hand.

Some interesting items to be found are a court cupboard with the royal crest of Charles II, an important Chippendale design display cabinet, and even a silver coaching horn. Decorating the walls are 18th- and 19th-century paintings and prints.

Winfield Winsor Antiques   73-111 El Paseo, Palm Desert, CA 92260   (619) 568-0970   Thursday-Monday: 11-4 and by appointment

Winfield Winsor

After 14 years as owner of an antiques firm in San Francisco's historic Jacson Square, Mr. Winsor recently opened his new shop in Palm Desert. The gallery's specialization is English country furniture dating from the late 17th century to the early 19th centuries no later than 1830. On hand are oak chests of drawers from the Cromwellian period, walnut and oak cricket tables from the early to mid-18th century, drop leaf oak and walnut dining and occasional tables, game tables, and consoles from the late 17th to the early 19th centuries. Various pieces of Chippendale, Sheraton, Hepplewhite and Thomas Hope are generally in stock. Faience (a tin-glazed earthenware especially from France), English ironstone (glazed white pottery), and Chinese export porcelain are strong areas of concentration. They range from early Chinese export and Japanese Imari and Arita ware to 18th- and early 19th-century English and continental ironstone and porcelain. Selections of plates, platters, tureens and urns are presented, in addition to Japanese screens and scrolls and Chinese tapestries.

Richard Yeakel

Richard Yeakel Antiques   1175 S. Coast Hwy., 1143 S. Coast Hwy., 1099 S. Coast Hwy., Laguna Beach, CA 92651   (714) 494-5526, 494-6667
Tuesday-Saturday: 8:30-4:30

Sixty miles south of Los Angeles in the seaside community of Laguna Beach are Richard Yeakel's three antique stores, each within a block of the other. The main store houses a fine collection of 17th- and 18th-century English, French, and nautical antiques. Another store specializes in fine American pieces, which include blockfront chests and furniture with the Wilhelm Schimmel eagle (a wooden eagle crafted by this traveling 19th-century wood-carver from Pennsylvania). The third store contains 15th- and 16th century Gothic and Renaissance period furniture, paintings, and tapestries.

The main store specializes in Queen Anne walnut furniture, such as a burl walnut grandfather clock signed and dated by Thomas Tompion and Edward Banger, who were among the earliest clockmakers of the period. One of the finest pieces on display is an early Queen Anne black japanned bureau bookcase with its original lacquer, dating about 1700. There is an array of George I and George II silver, including a pair of covered soup tureens by Paul Storr, and an offering of 18th-century Staffordshire pottery. There is also a section of jewelled Faberge of the late 19th century.

In the store housing the Gothic and Renaissance collection there is museum-quality furniture, such as a French Renaissance bed made during the reign of Henry IV (1580-1610). The large tapestries displayed are all 17th-century Flemish.

Gary E. Young

Gary E. Young   128 S. Commerce St., Centreville, MD 21617   (301) 758-2132   Daily: 10-5   Appointments encouraged

Located on the eastern shore of Maryland in the heart of historic Queen Anne's County, the firm has been in business for two generations. The large gallery in Centreville is located in a 3-story Federal house.

Dealing in both English and American period furniture, the shop is known for its specialization in library furnishings. There is usually a large selection of fine desks of all types, bookcases, architect's tables, reading stands, pedestal globes, and library steps. Rare books and fine bindings are also included.

A wide range of other antique furnishings are included and collector-quality furniture, selected for excellence of form, fine wood colour, and originality is emphasized throughout the nine showrooms. Secondary categories of emphasis are portrait miniatures on ivory, period brass, American and English animal, sporting, and marine art, barometers, bird decoys, and some folk art.

Primitive &
Ancient
Galleries

Primitive & Ancient Galleries

By Locations

California
Beverly Hills:
Franklin
San Francisco:
Willis
New Mexico
Santa Fe:
Bellas Artes
New York
New York City:
Pace Primitive
Texas
Houston:
Balene
Washington DC
Volta Pl.

By Specializations

African:
Balene
Franklin
Pace Primitive
Volta Pl.
Willis
American:
Balene
Bellas Artes
Oceanic:
Franklin
Willis
Pre-Columbian:
Balene
Bellas Artes

Balene, Inc.   2005 West Gray, Houston, TX 77019   (713) 523-2304   *Balene*
Monday-Friday: 12-5

Recently opened, the gallery represents a culmination for owner Balene
McCormick, who has been collecting primitive art for some 20 years. The
primitive art shown is from West Africa, the American Southwest, and
Pre-Columbian Mexico and Central America.

A show organized around the theme birds and beasts revealed marvelously
beaded, eerie elephant masks from the Cameroons; prehistoric pottery
900-1500 A.D. of the Southwest produced by vanished tribes such as the
Formile, Mimbers, Hohokam, Soccoro, and Tularosa; human- and
animal-shaped pottery jugs from the Colima people of Pre-Columbian
west-central-coast Mexico, and a number of other artifacts.

Additional items found in the gallery include excellent examples of
Southwestern Indian rugs and blankets ranging in vintage from 1850 to 1930;
turn-of-the-century Apache baskets; silver and turquoise concho belts,
bracelets and necklaces from the 1930s to the present; Acoma and Zia tribe
pottery from the historical past of the Southwest; a superb century-old Tlingit
weaving from the Pacific Northwest coast; a Mayan pottery head; and some
contemporary examples of Southwestern Indian pottery and basketmaking.

All of the items are of very high quality and beautifully displayed in a spare,
subdued setting. Although the price range is reflective of the rarity of many of
the pieces, a visit here is worthwhile for the student or aficionado of primitive
art as well as for the serious collector.

Bellas Artes   301 Garcia at Canyon Rd., Santa Fe, NM 87501   (505)   *Bellas Artes*
983-2745   Monday-Saturday: 10-5   January-March: closed Monday

Located in the historic district of Santa Fe, the gallery presents fine quality
handcrafted objects created through the ages. The collection of ceramics,
textiles, sculpture, and furniture represents diverse cultures and time periods,
yet demonstrates a striking harmony of style consistent with the handcrafted
tradition of the American Southwest.

Turn-of-the-century American arts, particularly those of the American
arts-and-crafts period (1880-1916) are always shown. The furniture of Gustav
Stickley, popularly known as mission furniture, includes Morris chairs, setties,
library tables, dining room tables, sideboards, rocking chairs, hall benches,

193

desks, and bookcases. American art pottery is represented by the Rookwood Pottery of Cincinnati, the Grueby Pottery of Boston, the Van Briggle Pottery of Colorado Springs, and the Newcomb Pottery of New Orleans, among others. The decorative arts of the period include Roycroft copperware, Dirk van Erp lamps, and objects from the Tiffany studios.

Textiles are always on display, including Pre-Columbian (600-1532 A.D.) Peruvian textiles ranging from complete ponchos to important fragments. Also seen are ancient Coptic textiles from Egypt and 19th century Oriental and Indonesian textiles, which harmonize with those of the Southwest. Antique kilims from the Balkans, Turkey, Iran, and the Caucasus provide an interesting contrast to the indigenous weavings usually seen in New Mexico.

Also on display are ancient figures, bowls, vases, and jewelry of various materials, including marble, bronze, terra cotta, gold, and silver. These objects, dating from the 8th century B.C. through the 4th century A.D., are Egyptian, Greek, Roman, Near Eastern, and Pre-Columbian in origin.

Harry A. Franklin

Harry A. Franklin Gallery   9601 Wilshire Blvd., Beverly Hills, CA 90210
(213) 271-9171   Tuesday-Saturday: 11-5 by appointment

For over 25 years the Franklins have maintained their reputation for integrity and museum-quality art. The gallery's specialty is traditional tribal sculpture—works made in traditional tribal settings for native use and not influenced by Western ideas. The focus is on sub-Saharan black Africa, that is, the savannahs and coastal lands of South Africa. Native Oceanic art of fine quality is also found here, as well as antiquities and Pre-Columbian artifacts.

The gallery is now in its second-generation of ownership under the direction of Valerie B. Franklin. As a former professor and writer in the area of primitive art, Ms. Franklin offers appraisal service as well as guidance in forming collections for individuals, public corporations, and institutions.

The Franklin Gallery is a source for many of the important collectors and museums in the country. The atmosphere of the gallery is one of friendly elegance where the newly interested and long-time collector can feel at home. All objects are guaranteed as to their authenticity.

Pace Primitive

Pace Primitive   32 E. 57th St., New York, NY 10022   (212) 421-3688
Tuesday-Saturday: 9:30-5:30   Summer: Monday-Friday 9:30-5:30

The gallery specializes in traditional sculpture from the art-producing areas of West and Central Africa. These masks and figures were created for native ceremonial and religious use. The objects are old, but not ancient. Their age depends greatly on their area of origin. The pieces are of museum quality and are of increasing rarity.

Among art-producing cultures whose sculpture can be found at the gallery are the Ashanti, Bambara, Baule, Chokwe, Dan, Dogon, Fang, Kota, Duba, Kongo, Ibon, Hemba, Lega, Mende, Reade, Senufo, Songye and Yoruba.

A permanent exhibition space is open to the public on the tenth floor, in which an assortment of African sculpure is displayed. Exhibitions are changed approximately every four weeks. The space is also used periodically for special exhibitions. Major exhibitions with elaborate catalogs are held on the second floor, such as shows of Yoruba beadwork and Yoruba sculpture of West Africa. Books and catalogs of African art are also available for sale.

Prices for authentic African art vary widely based on the relative importance and rarity of the piece, from a few thousand to over one hundred thousand dollars. Authenticity is the most important criteria for establishing value.

Yoruba beaded mask (Nigeria). Pace Primitive (New York).

Volta Place   Volta Place Gallery, Inc.   Volta Place & 33rd St., NW, Washington, DC, 20007   (202) 342-2003   Tuesday-Saturday: 12-6   August: by appointment

Located in historic Georgetown, the gallery specializes in authentic tribal art from Africa. Featured are ritual masks and statues including museum quality pieces. Fine examples of utilitarian arts and crafts such as containers, textiles, and jewelry are also displayed. This format enables the gallery to have a broad range of material that attracts collectors from beginners to museums.

An exhibition featured handmade jewelry and functional objects of the Masai and other peoples of eastern Africa. Beadwork made by the Masai is in bright rainbow colors and jewelry is worn according to age, social function, and station in life. Lawrence Ajanaku of Nigeria, an individual artist rare in African art, made costumes and headpieces. Each costume and mask depicts a specific character.

Other examples of ethnographic material are occasionally included, such as Mexican masks, Indonesian puppets, prehistoric American Indian pottery, and folk art. There are Kuba textiles from Zaire, Holo masks, Pygmy bark-cloth drawings, and ceramics from Kenya shown throughout the gallery.

James Willis   James Willis Gallery   109 Geary St., San Francisco, CA 94108   (415) 989-4485   Tuesday-Saturday: 11-5:30

Since 1971 the gallery has been specializing in the tribal arts of Africa, the Pacific, and Indonesia. The gallery emphasizes sculpture although fabrics and tribal jewelry are also exhibited. Wood sculpture from tribes in West Africa are always on hand. Work of the African tribe Fang on display includes statues, figures, fetishes, masks, and some architectural pieces. Yoruba wood carvings, masks, doors, house posts, and shrine and ancestral figures are displayed. One can see Bjenna terra cottas from Mali, which are mainly excavated pieces and figures.

Work from Indonesia is also featured in the gallery. There are artifacts, magical shaman staffs, and houns from the Batak tribe in Sumatra. Textiles from every island can be found, including shipcloth from Sumatra called prea, a ritual protective blanket in the ikat (dye-resistant) technique. Preas can also be found in the warp technique, which includes a supplemental thread creating an unusual design. There is a selection of excavated beads and metal work from Mesopotamia as well as some Oceanic material. Pottery in the form of large African pots and heads can be found. From New Mexico there are Santos, which are large crucifiction figures carved here by a religious sect, and from Naugaland in Northern India we find primitive jewelry.

Pre-Columbian textile detail of band, Huarmey
(800-1100 A.D.). Bellas Artes (Santa Fe, N.M.)

196

Tableware
Silver &
Porcelain
Galleries

Tableware, Silver & Porcelain Galleries

By Location

California
Los Angeles:
   English Heritage Silver
San Francisco:
   Argentum
Connecticut
Haddam:
   Hobart House
New York
New York City:
   Antique Porcelain Co.
   James II
   Kaplan
   Raphael
   Robinson
   Shrubsole
   Vandekar

By Specializations

Glass:
   Kaplan
Porcelain:
   Antique Porcelain Co.
   Kaplan
   Vandekar
Silver:
   Argentum
   English Heritage Silver
   Hobart House
   James II
   Raphael
   Robinson
   Shrubsole

Antique Porcelain Co.   48 E. 57th St., New York, NY 10022   (212) 758-2363   Monday-Friday: 9:30-6   August: closed first 3 weeks

The gallery was founded in London in 1946 by Hanns Weinberg who later opened a New York branch in 1947. His daughter and granddaughter now run the gallery, which deals in decorative arts of the 18th century. Of particular interest is the European porcelains of that period.

The early years of the major factories in Germany, France, England, and Italy are well represented both in tablewares and figurines. Meissen, a pottery factory established in Europe in 1710 for high-quality Chinese-influenced ware in mass production, is handled until 1755 with several works by the Germans Joseph Joachim Kaendler and Johann Gregor Herold who were working there in the 1720s. French Sevres, Chantilly, and Mennecy pieces are dealt with along with pieces from the early English factories of Chelsea, Derby, Bow, Longton Hall, and first period Worcester.

The gallery also maintains a display of the more primitive continental pottery, called faience, with examples from factories such as Delft, Brussels, Rouen, Marseilles, Erfurt, and Hoechst. Apart from ceramics, there are several pieces of 18th-century French furniture by renowned cabinet makers such as Carlin and Weisweiler. Also on hand is an important collection of 18th-century objects of virtue, gold boxes for snuff, scent or bodkins, and Renaissance jewelry spanning the 15th, 16th, and 17th centuries.

Argentum   1750 Union St., San Francisco, CA 94123   (415) 673-7509 Monday-Saturday: 11-5:30 or by appointment.

The core of the collection consists of English Georgian silver and American silver from the Colonial period to the early 20th century. Also available are examples of French and German 18th-century work as well as Spanish colonial pieces. Chinese export porcelain, American glass, and period paintings are displayed with the silver.

The large collection of English silver ranges in date from the 17th through the early 19th centuries, and always includes early spoons, 18th-century coffee pots and candlesticks, and representative pieces by the famous silversmiths such as Paul Storr and Hester Bateman. There are always a number of complete Georgian and early Victorian flatware services. American colonial and federal silver is a specialty, including items of regional interest as well as major pieces for museums and advanced collectors.

A small but fine collection of Chinese export porcelain is displayed along with examples of American glass, pewter, and brass. A varied selection of European and American paintings is also shown, as well as oriental rugs.

English Heritage Silver

English Heritage Silver   8840 Beverly Blvd., Los Angeles, CA 90048   (213) 550-8003/8004   Tuesday-Saturday: 11-6; Sunday: 12-5

Dealers Clive and Rita Blunt established the gallery concentrating on affordable English silver mainly of the Georgian period and specializing in spoons from 1500 on. The majority of the offerings are from 1700 to 1820, incorporating the period when English silver-smithing went through its great renaissance and development. Silver of the Britannia Standard, the highest standard in English Silver, is usually available. Among the names handled are 18th-century silversmith Paul de Lamerie, David Willaume and Peter Archambo. Silver of the middle Georgian period is represented by Samuel Woods, and the later Georgian period is well represented by the Bateman Family, the Hennells, Chawners, and Paul Storr, the leading Regency silversmith (1771-1844).

The gallery makes a specialization of collecting flatware sets from simple five-piece place settings for six people of mixed maker and date, up to straight boxed sets for 24 people sometimes incorporating as many as 300 individual pieces. Emphasis is also placed on salts, casters used for sprinkling condiments, and cake baskets. A number of silver pieces are displayed in English furniture primarily from the period 1760-1820.

Hobart House

Hobart House   Saybrook Rd., Rte. 9A, Haddam, CN 06438   (203) 345-2525 By appointment.

Founded in 1965, the gallery is located in a historic Connecticut home built in 1691. Emphasis is placed on early English silver pieces prior to 1830, such as candlesticks, tea sets, salvers (serving dishes usually with small feet for putting hot plates on a table), tankards (large drinking cups with a single handle and often a hinged lid), and general hollowware. Accompanying the silver is a display of fine needlework, including early samplers. Both silver and needlework are on display at all times in the older portions of the house.

There is also an extensive collection of snuff boxes and tea caddy scoops. Blue Staffordshire dinnerware and 18th-century English porcelain are also on display. The paneled rooms of the house are set off by Oriental rugs, which are not for sale.

James II

James II Galleries, Ltd.   15 East 57th St., New York, NY 10022   (212) 355-7040   Monday-Saturday: 10-5:30   Mid-June—Mid-September: Monday-Friday 10-5:30

Founded in 1966 as an extension of James Robinson, the gallery offers an extensive range of 19th-century English antiques and concentrates on the unusual and amusing. Within this eclectic collection can be found Victorian silver plates, games, Scottish and pique jewelry, furniture, silver picture frames, glass, and a major collection of ironstone and brass. It is a shop for both whimsical and serious purchases. Its ambience is one of informality.

Everything made in Victorian times for the table is here in silver plate. The pieces to be found range from tiny berry spoons to oversized soup tureens. The more serious and important pieces of brass are concentrated in The Brass

Room. There are a few 17th-century pieces as well as a good collection of 18th- and 19th-century specimens.

Another important area of specialization is early English ironstone dinner services. Although the familiar Imari patterns and colors are to be found (soft shades of green, blue, yellow, and orange on Japanese porcelain imported to Europe in the 17th century), the focus is on the more unusual and rarer color combinations.

There is a unique collection of Georgian and Victorian cut-steel jewelry, Scottish agate-set silver jewelry, and the fine, rare Victorian pique pieces done by the French as well as the English jewelers in the mid-19th century.

Leo Kaplan Ltd.   910 Madison Ave., New York, NY 10021   (212) 249-6766   Monday-Saturday: 10-5:30   June-August: Monday-Friday 10-5:30

Leo Kaplan

Specializing in fine antiques and art objects of the 18th, 19th, and 20th centuries, the Kaplans have four primary collections. There is an excellent selection of antique and contemporary glass paperweights for the novice to the most advanced collector. The finest contemporary paperweights are exhibited at the gallery by such celebrated artists as Paul Stankard, Bob and Ray Banford, Debbie and Delmo Tarsitano, and Rick Ayotte.

Cameo glass of the art nouveau period is represented by an extensive selection of French and English glass pieces of the late 19th and early 20th centuries. From France you will see examples of the works of Galle, Daum, Muller, Le Gras, and others, and even rarer works of superior quality by Eugene Michel. A wide variety of pieces by Thomas Webb & Sons and Stevens and Williams make up the English cameo glass collection.

Russian enamels and porcelain, including works of art by Karl Faberge, make up another area of specialization. From the 1880s until the onset of the Russian Revolution, these gemlike enameled pieces are typical of the Pan-Slavic movement in Russia. Included in this collection are examples of delicate plique-a-jour enamel of the same period made in neighboring Scandinavian countries.

Finally, the shop specializes in fine 18th-century English porcelain, and 18th- and early 19th-century English pottery. Particularly charming are the Thomas Whieldon and Ralph Wood toby jugs, and the slightly later Pratt figures and cottages.

M. Raphael of London   1050 Second Ave., New York, NY 10022 (212) 838-0178   Monday-Saturday: 10-5

M. Raphael of London

The firm has been in business in New York for over 35 years specializing in 17th-, 18th-, and 19th-century silver from different countries, including England, Germany, France, and Italy as well as 18th-century United States. The inventory ranges from 1560 to 1890.

Always in stock are pieces by well-known English silversmiths, including Regency-style tureens and ink stands by Paul Storr, candlesticks by Paul de Lamerie, and teapots and tea caddies by Hester Bateman. Other items include selections of soup tureens, coffee and tea services, tankards (large drinking cups), candlesticks, salvers (serving dishes), and cups.

The firm carries German silver from such noted centers as Augsberg and Nuremberg as well as Hamburg, Frankfort, and Berlin. French pieces, including Empire silver of the early 19th century, consist of such items as

Meissen bell and stand (1728). Antique Porcelain Co. (New York).

Proshau tureen (1775). Earle D. Vandekar of Knightsbridge (New York).

coffee pots, pairs of candlesticks, wine tasters, and brandy bowls. American silver by different makers, including Paul Revere of Boston, comes from New York and Philadelphia as well.

Also on display is an assortment of objects of vertu (fine art objects), such as gold and silver boxes, Russian enamel figures, ivory statues, and rock crystal.

James Robinson, Inc.   15 East 57th St., New York, NY 10022   (212) 752-6166   Monday-Friday: 10-5:30 Saturday: 10:30-5 except July & August

James Robinson

Established in New York in 1912, the gallery specializes in antique silver and jewelry. The silverware is mostly English and concentrates on the Georgian Period (1714-1830). There are coffee sets, tea sets, and dessert services on hand. Also carried is porcelain of the period from the well-known English factories of Coalport, Minton, and Worcester, all decorated with the gaily painted flowers and fruits of the period. There is glassware from Waterford and Bristol as well. Decanters, glasses, and candlesticks are colored in deep blue, green, and purple.

Jewelry concentrates on the Victorian Period (1830-1900), which is characterized by the colorful stones used during that period. Work is all hand done and many pieces have very intricate designs using Gothic forms and combinations of classical forms. Tiaras, brooches, necklaces, bracelets, and rings are all made up of brightly colored stones in the shapes of animals, snakes, birds, rabbits, crescents, stars, and many other designs. There are also examples of art nouveau jewelry, which is characterized by natural forms, such as flowers and trees.

S. J. Shrubsole Corp.   104 E. 57th St., New York, NY 10022   (212) 753-8920   Monday-Friday: 9:30-5:30

S. J. Shrubsole

The gallery was established in 1912 and is currently being run by the fourth generation of the Shrubsoles. It specializes in 16th-, 17th-, and 18th-century English silver and early American silver. Shrubsole carries English tureens, meat dishes, candelabras, and everything to do with the table. American silversmiths such as Paul Revere, Jacob Hurd, and John Coney crafted such items as teaspoons, teapots, table services, porringers, candlesticks, trays, and mugs on display at the gallery.

Although the gallery focuses on antique silver, antique jewelry and antique glass can also be found. Victorian jewelry is featured with necklaces and bracelets in addition to brooches by the famed English jeweler of the period, Carol Guiliano, known for his goldwork and unique style.

English and Irish glass predominates in the form of decanters, goblets, wineglasses, and sometimes candlesticks.

Earle Vandekar of Knightsbridge, Inc.   15 E. 57th St., New York, NY 10022   (212) 308-2022   Monday-Friday: 9:30-5:30; Saturday: 10-4; Summer: closed Saturday

Earle Vandekar of Knightsbridge

The Vandekars, who have been in the ceramic business since 1913 in London, expanded their business into the United States by opening a gallery in Los Angeles several years ago. In 1982, they moved to New York, where they offer a stunning array of porcelain dating from the 18th and first quarter of the 19th centuries. The emphasis of their stock is Chinese export ceramics dating from the 17th, 18th, and early 19th centuries. Included are famille verte pieces (with green or yellow-green ground) from the K'ang-hsi period and famille rose pieces (with red or pink ground) from the Ch'ein-lung period. All forms are to be found ranging from tureens, large soup bowls, smaller versions for sauces and vegetables and an enormous array of plates, animals, figures, bowls, vases, and several complete dinner services. There is also a selection of English ceramics, including examples from the major factories including Worchester, Coalport, Derby and Chelsea. There is a fine array of Staffordshire, English delftware (earthenware with a white opaque tin glaze), and creamware (a cream-colored earthenware with a transparent lead glaze).

Other items at Vandekar's include 18th- and 19th-century Chinese cloisonne enameled animals and other figures, glass paintings, and chandeliers. Continental ceramics on display always include a selection of Meissen (hard paste porcelain), Sevres, (soft paste porcelain), and Paris ceramics. Also included are pieces of Dutch delft and continental faience (delftware) from France, Germany, Ireland, Scotland, and Scandinavia.

Appendices

A. The Best

Index